Literature and the Young Child

Second edition

Joan E Cass

Formerly Lecturer in Child Development
London University Institute of Education

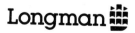
Longman

LONGMAN GROUP LIMITED
Longman House
Burnt Mill, Harlow, Essex CM20 2JE
and associated companies throughout the world

First published 1967
Second edition 1984
ISBN 0 582 36212 1 Paper edition
ISBN 0 582 36126 5 Cased edition

Printed in Hong Kong by
Sheck Wah Tong Printing Press Ltd

Dedication

To my Mother and Father and my friend and companion Beatrice
Arnold, who made my childhood so happy by the stories they told
me and the books and poetry they read to me. Although they are no
longer here to see this book, I dedicate it to them in remembrance
and love.

Contents

Introduction

I was lucky enough to be given a copy of the first edition of *Literature and the Young Child* when my children were small. I was already very interested indeed in children's books and was reviewing them regularly. I suppose you would say that I have always had a natural instinct for books and reading. Some people do, which is just as well because there are a great many children who miss out on the world books can open to them.

When, as a young mother, I started *BOOKS FOR YOUR CHILDREN* in the hope that it might spread good books further to those children, Joan Cass gave freely of her time, experience and culinary skills. We spent many meetings in her cottage expounding theories about children's literature, while she cooked superb suppers for us all. For Joan is an essentially practical person. No one has a greater imaginative response to literature, but she combines this with an understanding of children that takes into account their day to day needs.

In the early days of *BOOKS FOR YOUR CHILDREN* the most difficult question we were ever asked was 'Why?' Why read books at all? Children can perfectly well grow up with only basic reading ability, especially nowadays with the magic video and TV box in the corner. It is so easy to find other causes which, on the face of it, seem more important than literature. But there is nothing more important than encouraging the flight of the imaginations of children. They are already free. Too often they become fettered by outside pressures, even when they are quite young. Joan Cass's reply to the question 'Why should children read books at all' is quite simply, 'Think of all they will miss if they don't.'

My children are now almost grown up. What I recognised by instinct to be true in *Literature and the Young Child* when they were small, I can now confirm by experience. With literature, as with every other department in life, children need to be directed. There is no better starting point for parents and teachers than this book.

ANNE WOOD
Editor, *Books for Your Children* magazine

Preface

This book is written for parents and teachers, or in fact anyone who reads and tells stories and poetry to young children or who shares the delights of picture books with them.

It is sometimes difficult to know what to choose from the wealth of material available today and we want to select wisely and provide young children with the best. We are all individuals and we have our own special needs, our likes and dislikes, and this is as true of boys and girls as it is of adults.

On the other hand, children do go through stages in their growth and development when certain kinds of stories, poems and picture books will appeal more than others.

In the following pages I have tried to show what children round about two to seven or eight want and enjoy and how we can best satisfy their pleasure in books by selecting those which not only possess quality, but are also ones they will like.

Author's Acknowledgements

There are always people one wants to thank at the beginning of a book even though they may not necessarily agree with all one has written.

Many of them, of course, are unknown and unnameable: children who have listened to the stories one has told, laughed and shown pleasure in them; parents, students, teachers, who have asked a question or given an example which has stimulated and challenged one's own thinking.

Two people, particularly in their capacity as personal friends and with the experience too of a professional life, have read the manuscript and made comments and suggestions. Kathleen Lade and Winifred Wallace have provided both encouragement and advice which I have found extremely helpful, and I am very grateful to them both for all they have done. I would like to thank Iris Ritchie very much for typing the manuscript. Last, but not least, I would like to thank Anne Wood for her delightful introduction.

Acknowledgements

We should like to thank the following for permission to reproduce illustrations:

Abelard-Schuman Ltd: page 25, illustration by William Stobbs for Joan Cass, *The Cat Show*; Faber and Faber Ltd: page 37, illustration by Shirley Hughes for Sara and Stephen Corrin, *Stories for Seven-Year-Olds*; Hamish Hamilton Ltd: page 73, illustration by Robert Lawson for Munro Leaf, *The Story of Ferdinand*; Oxford University Press: pages 3 and 50, woodcuts by Joan Hassall for Iona and Peter Opie, *The Oxford Nursery Rhyme Book*; Frederick Warne and Co Ltd: page 63, illustration by L. Leslie Brooke for *Johnny Crow's Garden*.

We are grateful to the following for permission to reproduce copyright material:

the proprietors of *The Countryman* for lines from 'The Butterfly' by S. Thomas Ansell; the author's agents and Michael Joseph for lines from '*Silver, Sand and Snow*' by Eleanor Farjeon; the author's agent for an extract from *Collected Essays* by Graham Greene, The Bodley Head Ltd (1951); the Literary Trustees of Walter de la Mare and The Society of Authors as their representatives for lines from '*Once*' by Walter de la Mare.

The photograph on the cover is by Sally and Richard Greenhill

The Lost Childhood

'Perhaps it is only in childhood that books have any deep influence on our lives. In later life we admire, we are entertained, we may modify some views we already hold, but we are more likely to find in books merely a confirmation of what is in our minds already; as in a love affair it is our own features that we see reflected flatteringly back. But in childhood all books are books of divination, telling us about the future, and like the fortune teller who sees a long journey in the cards or death by water they influence the future. I suppose that is why books excite us so much. What do we ever get nowadays from reading to equal the excitement and the revelation in those first fourteen years.

.   .   .

No, it is in those early years that I would look for the crisis the moment when life took a new slant in its journey towards death.'

Graham Greene

1
First Thoughts

Man is a thought-adventurer. He has thought his way down the far ages. He used to think in little images of wood or stone. Then in hieroglyphs on obelisks and clay rolls and papyrus. Now he thinks in books between two covers.

D. H. Lawrence

I shall always remember with excitement and delight some of my very first books and the extraordinary pleasure they gave me.

There were two picture books especially, which I shall never forget, for they were associated in my mind with all the love and comfort of home. They were both quite ordinary little books; one had pictures of children at home, playing with their dolls, putting them to bed, looking after them, having tea parties. The predominant colour in the pictures was a wonderful violet blue, such a glorious colour, or so it seemed to me, that I can see it as clearly today as I did when I first turned the pages as a child.

The other book was an oblong linen one with large coloured pictures of boys and girls playing out of doors. It showed perpetual summer with bright, green grass, distant trees and a smooth blue sky. In the picture I remember most clearly all the children were holding hands in a ring as if they were about to play a game.

Both these books were associated in my mind with happiness and security, for they were the basis of a warm and loving relationship. I looked at them first with a dearly loved adult and together we shared the pictures and the very simple story.

This sharing seems to me very important as far as all young children are concerned; it certainly mattered to me as a child. Books were not merely a collection of stories and pictures; they were part and parcel of the very fabric of my life – looked at, talked about and brooded over with those I loved and so were associated in my mind, not only with their contents, but also with the warmth, the comfort and the belongingness of my own treasured family.

Looking back on these particular books as an adult they seem to me also, perhaps, to symbolise a child's two worlds, the world of home, and the world outside, both so meaningful. One book depicted all the ordinary domestic household details which are so much part of a young child's early environment, while in the second book, one saw the world beyond home – the grass, the trees, the sky and other children; scenes a little less secure and familiar yet, nevertheless, excitingly new; a part of an expanding world. I wonder if I remember these two books so vividly for this reason.

All children, I am sure, should be able to look back on their first remembered books with pleasure, associating them with affectionate and trusted adults able and ready to spare the time for the individual attention so necessary for the happiness of the young child.

At the very early stages it is, of course, the adult who is the provider of books; whether as parents, relatives, substitute parents or teachers, we do the choosing and buying, we are the people who give children the books they are going to look at. It is little use, therefore, complaining of the poor reading tastes of the older boy and girl if, from babyhood onwards, children have been given a diet of the tawdry and the second-rate, for early impressions regarding books are as vital as early impressions on anything else. Books must be enjoyed by children, otherwise they will soon be discarded. And if, as adults, we have built up feelings of anxiety and apprehension in relation to the actual skills of learning to read, so that children experience a sense of failure and dislike whenever a book is put into their hands, we shall have done the young irreparable harm. Our task, therefore, is to make books and stories so enchanting to children they cannot resist them. Then, slowly and gradually, they will begin to want to understand the printed word for themselves.

Of course, not all children will like the same stories and we do not want them to accept blindly everything that is handed out to them. A book needs to be significant to the person who is reading it, and we hope children will gradually discover for themselves what emotional and intellectual experiences others have had that can best help and serve them.

Nevertheless, they will need our aid in learning to discriminate from the vast masses of books available so that they can find those best suited to their needs. We should be ready, therefore, with the right book at the right moment, whether it is Beatrix Potter's *Peter Rabbit*, Hans Andersen's *Fairy Tales* or *The Adventures of Robin Hood*.

We should know too, enough about the stages that children, in spite of individual differences, go through, to be able to give them something they can enjoy.

It is important to remember that children are not born with inherent good taste. Left entirely to their own devices with such an enormous number of books available, they can waste a great deal of time on very mediocre material. Childhood does not last for ever, and if a book is not discovered at the appropriate stage it may never be read or seen at all. This can mean that enchanting and worthwile books are missed altogether.

2

Picture Books and their Illustrations

Alice was beginning to get very tired of sitting by her sister on the bank, and having nothing to do; once or twice she had peeped into the book her sister was reading, but it had no pictures or conversation in it, 'and what is the use of a book' thought Alice, 'without pictures or conversation'.

Lewis Carroll

Through the ages man has developed the capacity to use shapes symbolically to suggest ideas and concepts in pictures and writing. Everyone is so familiar with this phenomenon that it is sometimes forgotten that these skills have to be learnt by children. The more abstract and remote these shapes are, and the more complex the ideas which they convey, the more difficult children will find them to understand.

Obviously a child's response to what he sees will depend on the maturation of his brain. Although one cannot bypass the stages of growth, a stimulating environment encourages children to develop more rapidly. The child who is denied food for his bodily needs will grow more slowly, taking longer to perform those actions which are natural to childhood, and the same principle applies to mental growth. They can be helped or hindered by the environment in which they find themselves. This will include the stimulation and interest of other human beings, for children do not develop in isolation. They need the wise and loving care of adults, and contacts with other children.

It is not necessary here to go into a detailed description of the growth of perception in young children, but there are some practical points that should be borne in mind. Obviously, there are phases through which a child passes before the objects and scenes he sees in his picture books will have meaning for him.

Arnold Gesell, who was the Director of the Clinic of Child Development at Yale University and carried out, with a team of workers, a systematic developmental research programme studying the behaviour and reactions of young children suggests that between eighteen months and two years, children enjoy picking out familiar objects in pictures and patting and stroking them. They still, however, treat books in a very light-hearted, casual fashion and will tear or scribble on them if unsupervised. Round about the ages of two or three most children recognize simple objects in pictures and can find them in a fairly complicated illustration. At about 2·6 the Terman Merrill Intelligence Test[1] expects a child to be able to distinguish six simple objects on a card and name them, and about 3·6, to describe very briefly what he can see in three different pictures.

Children also tend at this age to recognize objects in pictures whatever their position in space; this means that they will sometimes look at their picture books upside-down and still be able to name the things that are there. This tendency to ignore spatial orientation means that they do not always analyse what they see and so do not separate the important from the unimportant; that is why they will often pick out some apparently trivial object in a picture with great excitement and interest. Many two-year-olds, for example, will at first be confused if a picture shows only part of a thing – the bonnet of a car, or the front legs of an animal. Alan aged 2·2 was quite upset as he looked at Marjorie Flack's *Angus Lost*, which shows just the front wheels of a motor car and the two back legs of a dog vanishing off the page, and kept murmuring to himself rather sadly, 'Poor thing, all broke'.

Because of this failure to analyse children do not, until about 4 to 4·6, recognize a series of actions in different pictures; they see each one separate from the rest. Even children of six and seven often find sudden changes of period and background difficult to grasp as they do not necessarily see the relationship between the two.

If a picture has a meaning that is not actually shown, young

[1] The Terman Merrill Intelligence Test is a standard test used for the evaluation of intellectual status. It is useful in that it helps us to compare a child's intellectual level, i.e. his brightness or dullness in comparison with other children of his age, only, however, in relation to this particular test.

children will not understand what is implied. It is not until a child is past seven that the Terman Merrill Intelligence Test expects the average boy or girl to interpet the picture of a telegraph boy whose cycle has lost a wheel and who is waving to a passing car to ask for a lift.

Obviously it will be the familiar in a picture that will engage a child's attention first. Some illustrators of picture books appear to forget this and to live in the past when houses, furniture, clothes, etc., were very different from today. Children like to see familiar objects in their pictures, boys and girls wearing garments like themselves, and houses furnished with things they can recognize: television sets, refrigerators, gas and electric cookers.

Colour is an important factor in books and young children generally choose those with coloured pictures in preference to black-and-white unless the book happens to be one containing a well-loved story. Red is generally the first colour to be recognized and chosen, followed by yellow, blue and green. By five, blue is often chosen first. Children also tend to associate certain colours with certain objects – a yellow sun, a blue sky, green grass and brown tree trunks. Colours, too, can be soothing or disturbing and the frightening quality of a picture can be enhanced if it is shown in blacks, dark purples and dark blues.

Colour which is blurred and unevenly applied in pictures so that it spills over the outline of the different objects and scenes is disliked by children and they often comment upon it; they prefer things to be neat and tidy if they are meant to be so.

It is thought that children probably do not observe colours accurately until they can name them and match the four primary colours correctly at about four.[1] On the other hand they are attracted by the bright, primary colours earlier, even if their response is merely one of primitive emotional excitement. About $7\frac{1}{2}$ per cent of the male population suffer from some type of colour-blindness. Colour-blindness is a sex-linked hereditary characteristic transmitted by the female to the male; it is rare to find this defect in women.

Part of the whole process of learning in young children is classify-

[1] Mary D. Sheridan, *The Development Progress of Infants and Young Children*, H.M.S.O.

ing objects, learning that an object looks different when it is seen in a different position or far away, and realising that the shape seen with the eyes is the same as that felt with the hands. As Susan Isaacs points out in her essay on 'The Nursery School' [1]:

> The child is always trying to see things better, to make out the differences between table and chair, cup and spoon, apple and orange, the flowers and the birds, the fire and the sun, the dog and the cat, the smiles and frowns of his mother, and the faces of this person and that. His pursuit of these differences leads to the maturing of his sense of discrimination and the storing of his mind with external knowledge.

Children under six or seven tend to see 'wholes', so figures in pictures need to be strong and clear in outline, otherwise they may appear just as a lot of unrelated detail. Nor must the value of the spoken word be forgotten in relation to children's looking. The tendency nowadays to attach importance to visual aids in education, showing children pictures, diagrams, etc., needs to be considered in relation to the way in which they see and remember things.

Professor M. D. Vernon, in her book *The Psychology of Perception*, points out that showing particular pictures of scenes or incidents may not, by themselves, give children under eleven any really clear idea of what is happening. They may only be confused by unfamiliar costumes, settings, and small details. Just showing the pictures, therefore, is not enough; they must be talked about and discussed by the children and the adult. The same thing applies to films and television programmes: what is actually said is of the greatest importance. Professor Vernon also suggests that there is evidence to show that if children's emotions are aroused, 'their recollections may be distorted in that information toward which they are favourable is over-emphasized, whereas that which arouses their dislike or hostility may be either ignored or forgotten'.

It is often difficult to define the qualities in a satisfying illustration in a children's book and those qualities which are unsuitable are sometimes easier to pinpoint and describe. Art is, of course, a communication and in a picture book for a child the illustrator,

---

[1] Susan Isaacs, *Childhood and After. Some Essays and Clinical Studies*, Routledge & Kegan Paul.

whether in colour or line, is helping to interpret and retell the story that has been written, so that once the book has been read to the child he can reread the tale for himself through the pictures. The illustrator will also add to his pictures those extra little details, unmentioned in the text, the spoon by the honey jar, the daisies on the grass, the chintz curtains at the windows, which children look for and find so entrancing. Pictures in a book can, and do, exist in their own right and there are occasions when the story they retell is a rather flimsy and unsubstantial affair. Children will then just enjoy feasting their eyes on exciting scenes and colours. Generally speaking, however, in a true picture book the illustrations are not there just to bolster up a rather meaningless little story. Boys and girls certainly need good illustrations but an interesting dramatic story that is echoed by the pictures so that both are of value makes a more satisfactory book in the long run.

As children get older this simple retelling of a tale through pictures is not so necessary; the words will do this. Yet pictures are often an exciting and much needed addition, particularly for the slower child. They may show some special background or scene, or add a dramatic and moving quality which can excite children, who suddenly discover something new in the story they had not thought of for themselves.

For young children a picture needs to spring to life out of the pages of their picture books with all the spontaneous freshness and intensity which is a part of themselves, while at the same time the artist must use all the skill, experience, and originality that he possesses to enchant and woo them. Because children bring to what they see their own fresh imaginations they do not discriminate between what is good and bad. They willingly accept what we give them, particularly the young child, who tends to expect the adult on whom he is so dependent to be all-loving and giving. At times, it is true, he may look at our gifts with a certain amount of puzzlement, anxiety and questioning, but he still accepts them with unfailing trust.

This lack of any real critical faculty means that young children can all too easily be imposed on, and the shoddy, the cheap, and the second-rate can be handed out to them indiscriminately, and be innocently enjoyed.

Every creative artist will, of course, speak to children in his own particular idiom, and each one will have something a little different to say in the interpretation of the story he is illustrating. If, however, a child is going to understand what the picture is telling him, the artist must know something about the way in which children see the world and feel about the people, animals and objects in it; though pictures, like stories, can speak to children at more than one level, containing as it were hidden secrets, which only gradually reveal themselves. The emotion that is conveyed by a picture, whether it is gaiety, compassion, tenderness, anger or fear, must be genuine and devoid of sentimentality and depicted in such a way that a child can cope with and interpret its meaning, either consciously or unconsciously, for his own needs and purposes.

It is not easy to know what sort of pictures will frighten individual boys and girls and some people feel that aggression, hostility and hate as shown in a picture help children to come to terms with these feelings in themselves. Children certainly need to do this, but probably do it more effectively in an active way, especially at the under five level. Thus, it is in their own self-chosen, spontaneous play that these feelings probably find most suitable and satisfying outlets which can be worked through and understood; certainly sadism, torture and macabre horror have no place in children's pictures.

It can happen, too, that illustrations conceived by adults may introduce elements that are haunting and fear-provoking, and which children themselves would not have envisaged in this way. The picture book of *The Three Robbers*, with its sombre, dark colours and sinister characters may alarm some children, though others will enjoy it. The story of *The Wolf and the Seven Little Kids*, by the Brothers Grimm, dramatically illustrated by Felix Hoffman, shows pictures in which the wolf is cut open by the mother goat and then filled up with stones to replace the kids he had swallowed. He is then carefully sewn up with a long needle and thread. These pictures are colourful and exciting but they may easily disturb some children who are already anxious about what happens inside people's 'tummies' and where babies come from. Thus their own somewhat disturbing birth fantasies are echoed in the pictures without any reassuring comfort. These feelings may not be experienced by every child. Many will find the book intriguing and revel in gazing at the illustrations, and the story is a very popular one with children.

It is sometimes better to tell young children certain stories without showing them pictures at all, then the frightening elements are not over-emphasized.

Some illustrations in children's books are, unfortunately, reminiscent of the poorer advertisements one sees, where a conventional, unreal world is shown full of conventional, unreal human beings. Boys, girls and adults gaze from the pages with vacant faces, and everyone looks exactly the same, completely devoid of character and personality.

Richard Hoggart in his book *The Uses of Literacy*, in writing about modern pin-ups, says: 'At first they look extremely suggestive and in some ways they are. And yet they are strangely ersatz. They inhabit regions so stylised, so pasteurised, that the real physical quality has left them.... Everything has been stripped to a limited range of visual suggestion.' He then goes on to compare these ersatz creatures with the reality of, say, a Degas dancer.

This kind of thing can happen in a slightly different way in illustrations in children's books, when all the liveliness, individuality and feeling that human beings possess is somehow smoothed away to an arid, insipid sameness. Obviously, if in the story the characters laugh, cry, look grubby and untidy as children often do, this should be shown. Lines, which are the marks of feeling and maturity on a face, are often left out and a strange, unnatural adult looks at the child without emotion or expression.

Equally unpleasing are the Mabel Lucy Attwell prototypes: pert, rather vulgar-looking children with fat, flabby limbs, arch eyebrows and sweeping lashes, or some of the more modern ones where boys and girls appear with enormous heads, tiny bodies and no discernible mouths, all looking repulsively deformed.

There are of course picture books containing lively, interesting and natural children and adults such as the Swedish series, *Christmas at Bullerby, Cherry Time at Bullerby* by Astrid Lindgren, illustrated by Ilon Wickland, or *Lucy and Tom's Day* written and illustrated by Shirley Hughes.

Animals, too, are sometimes shown as ugly and grotesque, with limbs and bodies distorted for no functional purpose, so that they lose their animal characteristics altogether. Whereas creatures as real as William Stobbs's superb cats in my cat books[1] or Robert Lawson's illustrations to Munro Leaf's *The Story of Ferdinand the Bull*, show how expressive such animals can be and yet retain their natural characteristics.

An artist should not only capture the mood and feeling of a story; he must also be careful not to confuse children by a sudden departure from the text. The indifferent artist, or publisher for that matter, sometimes does not even ensure that his scenes and colours fit the tale or that the right picture is next to the incident that it is supposed to illustrate.

Simple information in a story picture book should always be accurate and in *Spring is a New Beginning*, Joan Walsh Anglund suggests, in both her descriptions and illustrations, that violets, Easter eggs, and all the pleasures of Spring include the gathering of wild strawberries; alas, wild strawberries are a summer fruit and children who look for them among the Spring flowers will be sadly disappointed.

Alphabet books are not, as a rule, completely successful, as young children are neither ready for nor interested in letters and words at the age for which these books are written. So often, too, the artist finds difficulty in discovering new words for the letters, and in order to be original, introduces objects that are completely divorced from young children's limited experience.

Reproductions from cartoons do not make good picture books and even Walt Disney's more attractive ones, when removed from their appropriate setting to become 'stills', look lifeless and unnatural. The artist who tries to draw in the way the child does is also doomed to failure – children do it so much better. We obviously want children to experience a variety of styles and media in their picture books: water-colour, oil, pastel, pen and ink, lithograph etc., and a variety of different interpretations by different artists.

Studies of children's preferences tend to show that they enjoy realistic, stylised, near abstract and caricature, provided there is unity and harmony between the story and the picture, each com-

---

[1] Joan Cass, *The Cat Thief, The Cat Show, Blossom Finds a Home, The Canal Trip*. Abelard-Schuman.

plementing and fitting the other.[1] There is, for example, the delightful intimacy of Beatrix Potter's illustrations with their soft pastel colours and the loving accuracy of her country scenes and animals. Edward Ardizonne in picture books such as *Little Tim and the Brave Sea Captain, Tim and Charlotte Go to Sea*, with his vigorous, sketchy quality, gives children the feeling that the very spirit of the scene has been snatched from a moment in time and held for ever in colour and line. Only the essential qualities have been seized on at the moment of impact so that the adventures of his characters are high-lighted for ever in time and space.

Nothing could be more expressive or individual than Leslie Brooke's illustrations to his *Johnny Crow Picture Books*. The humorous expressions and dramatic gestures of his animals, 'The pig who danced a jig' and 'The beaver who had a fever' bring their personalities to life in an unforgettable way. Kathleen Hale in her *Orlando* series about a marmalade cat and his family, with their vivid colour and sophisticated detail, delight many children; while Ludwig Bemelmans conveys in his picture books about 'Madeline' not only the feel and flavour of Paris, but the mischievous behaviour of this incorrigible and exuberant little girl. For the younger child of 2 or $2\frac{1}{2}$ simplicity of scene and clear cut figures and not too much detail is important. On the other hand, young children love ordinary commercial catalogues containing pictures of familiar household goods, furniture, kitchen utensils – things they see their mothers using about the house. Janet and Allan Ahlberg's 'The Baby Catalogue' (Kestrel) is a delightful example of this and of the everyday life a child sees; while The Bruna Books (Methuen) are pleasing examples of very simple pictures and text.

On the whole, photographs are less popular than original illustrations though there are exceptions.

The skilful artist will use all sorts of devices to create atmosphere and mood, including the use of colour and space, the size of the pictures, their arrangement and format. Some picture books produce variety by interweaving pictures and text on the same page. Virginia Lee Burton's *The Little House* arranges some of the type to

[1] Morton S. Maeter, 'Children's Preferences for Illustrative Materials', *Journal of Educational Research* 41, pp. 378–85, January, 1948.

follow the pattern of a winding road which appears in her illustrations. But print actually superimposed on a picture is generally found to be confusing, both to the reader and non-reader.

There is a definite preference for pictures placed on the righthand side of the page, and in the advertising world space in newspapers and magazines costs more if the righthand page is taken.

The end-papers and the title-page add to the charm of a book, while the dust cover is probably the first thing both children and adults notice and so will influence their choice. Claire Rayner in an article in the December 1963 number of *Design* stresses the importance of the actual physical properties of a book.

> The feel of a book and the way it handles, are important to a child. Something that is fragile can distress him a great deal, for he needs to feel that his environment is strong and secure. Something that breaks easily is frightening because it diminishes his trust in the physical world. So a good book from a child's standpoint is strong and will hold its shape . . . the paper pages should be bound together in such a way that the binding will hold them firmly but at the same time will allow the book to be opened flat.

Charlotte S. Huck and Doris A. Young in their book *Children's Literature in the Elementary School* suggest that the paper used in a children's picture book should be dull so that it does not reflect the light; it should be bound in cloth, side sewn and have soil resistant, washable covers.

Rag books for the very young, although made of material which is hard to tear, soon become limp and floppy and although they can be starched, this is a real effort for the busy mother.

Children appear to enjoy books of different sizes, small, medium and large and in some picture books the shape actually suggests the content.

Many young children approach their early picture books as if the characters portrayed were almost alive and they will kiss or stroke a favourite animal or person. Perhaps, just as some modern artists build up their pictures with actual materials – sand, hessian, concrete; surfaces that can be felt – so a pig made of pale pink velvet, or a little girl with a silk frock that children can touch, may not be wholly inappropriate in picture books.

13

'Pop-up' books have the fascination of miniature theatres, but they are not very suitable for young children as they are so easily torn by exploring fingers.

Although the young child is really concerned with the pictures, he will be aware, to some extent, of the type faces to which he is exposed and the older child will, of course, be even more affected when he is starting to read. If the type face is too large it tends to attract the eye to individual letters rather than to the word pattern. The same applies to the space between the lines: if too wide this makes for lack of continuity, while if lines are too close together children can inadvertently read the same line twice. If the line is too long children are confused in finding the next; if too short it stops them taking in long phrases; and those of us who never read comics when we were children, find the very short phrases in the balloons quite tiring to read. Margins of about an inch appear to be the most suitable, as a very narrow one produces visual fatigue. There are differences of opinion on which is the most suitable type face – the serif (a, b, c, d) or the sans serif (a, b, c, d).

There is no particular evidence to support the sans serif. It is claimed that it is similar to children's own writing; that it helps boys and girls to learn the essential structure of the letters in their simplest form, and that serifs are unfunctional. Sir Cyril Burt's investigations,[1] however, seemed to indicate the reverse. Serifs helped the visual speed of the eye, its movement along the line and the recognition of the pattern of the word.

In daily life children are going to meet all sorts of written material on tins, food packets, birthday cards, letters, notices and posters in shops and streets, so a lack of uniformity has its uses. It must be remembered, too, that picture story books should not be confused with first reading books though even here type faces vary.

Most picture books are meant to be read aloud to children and their print, style and vocabulary are thus designed. First reading books, on the other hand, are concerned with children's reading ability level and therefore their print, as well as their style and vocabulary are geared to this purpose. This means that their style tends to be very simple and their word content controlled. Such

[1] *A Psychological Study of Typography*, CUP.

books are cheap to buy; children read them quickly and then discard them. They serve their purpose and are then forgotten and finished with. Picture story books, on the other hand, are often treasured possessions, kept for years and handed down from parents to children.

Because children are travellers, setting out on voyages of discovery, picture books can offer them one of the earliest and most enchanting ways of extending their experience of the world. Poring over their picture books they can behold the delight of new places and new people, of strange birds and beasts, of lands very different from their own. 'Magic casements' are opened for them, looking out over the vastness of the earth with its perpetual promise of new surprises.

3

What Sort of Stories?

And books are yours
Within whose silent chambers treasure lies
Preserved from age to age.
Wordsworth

'What's it about, that's what I want to know', said the small boy in the library, fingering the pages of a story book; and that is what most people wonder when they pick up a book from the shelves to look at, borrow or buy. 'What will the tale tell me?'

The kinds of stories that different people enjoy will depend on a variety of things: their ages, their environments, their experiences, interests and moods. Whatever age we happen to be, or whatever experiences we happen to have had, we all demand that our books tell us a story in which something happens; we want a dramatic plot because drama, however simple, is the very stuff of life. There are not, of course, nearly enough different plots to go round, particularly when one considers the millions of books that have been written and yet, in spite of this, every book that is worth reading or looking at is unique in its own way.

What really makes every story a new one, even if it is fairly simple, is the characters in it. The way they develop and behave, how they feel and think, and their reactions to different experiences give the story its drama and make things happen. If the characters are quite unsubstantial, shadowy figures, untouched by the things that happen to them, oblivious to the passing of time, remaining immature from the first page to the last, then the story will be unreal and unsatisfying. Of course, one does not expect an individual character to change completely in a very short space of time. The bad little boy or girl who suddenly becomes exceedingly good in a very few sentences never really rings true, for growth is a slow process.

The development of the characters, however, is fascinating and

16

the longer the tale, the more complex they tend to become. So, one sees not only the effects of human beings on one another, but also the way in which they behave and approach the experiences of life: the motives that move them, the strength and complexity of their feelings and their inner conflicts.

This may sound rather far-fetched in considering stories for young children, but they, too, are profoundly interested in relationships at a very basic but fundamental level. They want to know about life, and life is made up of human beings: themselves and other people. One of the difficulties in writing stories for young children is to make the characters come to life, so that what they do is the result of what they are, in a very short space of time, without creating people so complex as to be beyond the understanding of children. In many of the first stories we tell to young children the characters appear to represent very simple virtues or vices – the loving mother, the good father, the naughty kitten, etc., and so they tend to be 'types' playing a simple part in a homely incident. Yet even at this first stage a real person can emerge and Mary, in William Nicholson's *The Pirate Twins*, with the help of the delightful pictures comes to life as a person of undoubted character.

Perhaps the writer who springs to mind most vividly as the creator of living personalities for really young children is Beatrix Potter. First of all, the drama in her stories – and there is plenty of it – arises as the direct result of what her characters are and how they feel and act. Jemima Puddleduck, that endearing, obstinate, rather credulous little duck, has just the sort of adventures that someone of her nature would have. So, of course, do Peter Rabbit and Tom Kitten. Often in a single sentence Beatrix Potter can sum up for children the personality of the animal she is writing about. Yet she does not bewilder children or confuse them with too much detail, providing just those touches that bring everyone to life.

For the older child who can listen to a longer story it is not so difficult to show character development, but even here, without real thought, it is only too easy to create lifeless dummies.

Children are primarily interested in action. What they want to know is how the person or animal will behave under certain circumstances; therefore they must do things to show the sort of people they are.

Now in spite of the fact that plot and personality development cannot really be separated in stories for young children, particularly those under five, it is important that the subject matter of the tale is one that is within their understanding and experience. Stories that are read and told to children can seem very real indeed; like us, they identify themselves with the people in the tales they hear.

At the preschool stage, therefore, it is a mistake to tell boys and girls stories of parents who desert and reject their children – like 'Hansel and Gretel' or 'The Babes in the Wood'. Every young child needs the constant reassurance of being loved and wanted by either his parents or substitute parents and even to hear about being pushed out at this stage is often too terrifyingly real; all children have fantasies of losing the love of those they need most. It is true, of course, that this has actually happened to some children and they will have to learn to accept it, but at this age it is rather like rubbing salt into a wound that really needs soothing and healing. Such stories can be accepted and enjoyed when children get a little older, fantasy and reality have sorted themselves out and boys and girls are more assured of their special place in the family. Meantime, kind and loving parents who do the right things in stories find a real echo in young children's hearts, for this is what they want and need.

All this is very closely linked, too, with the grown-up world of real things, which is a topic full of meaning to young children. Mothers at home with all their round of exciting domestic activities; cooking and cleaning, washing and sweeping, shopping and visiting. Fathers who do brave and clever things in the world outside the home; mending roads, driving buses, flying planes, directing the traffic. All these things and many more are full of romance and adventure to the young child who is very deeply concerned with discovering all he can about the world and the people in it. He needs, too, to feel part of the good, brave, clever things that grown-up people are able to do, and in fantasy to share in helping to mend and clean and put the bad things right.

Then there are the events in which children themselves take part, both within the family and beyond it: parties and picnics, holidays and expeditions, bus rides and train journeys. Quite ordinary things, but an important part of living.

Young children, of course, do not mind stories about boys, girls

18

and animals who are naughty and get punished for their wrong-doing. In fact, as we all do, they get a vicarious enjoyment in hearing about bad behaviour which they themselves would like to indulge in, and probably do sometimes. Naturally the punishment meted out to the wrong-doer in the story should be neither excessive nor sadistic but just enough for the child to get that satisfied feeling that justice has been done.

The over-five also has strong feelings about punishing the wrong-doer but he has not really sorted out his ideas of right and wrong and so is not clear about who should be punished and how severe such punishment should be.

Between about 5 and $6\frac{1}{2}$ it is not so much the motive that counts in an act as the actual damage done. So, to break a great many dishes by accident because the victim did not know they were there, is much worse than to break one through disobedience or naughtiness. Stealing from kings and queens or really important people also always seems much worse to children than taking things from ordinary people, so the punishments that are envisaged for those who rob royalty are very severe – hanging being fairly popular or, as one six-year-old remarked, 'I'd put them on a bonfire and burn them and burn them till their blood ran out'.

Children themselves do not want their own misdeeds discovered and often do not even think they have done anything wrong unless they are caught. This is because naughtiness is closely linked with parental approval and disapproval and if a parent is not angry because the child's behaviour has remained undetected then, obviously, it cannot be really bad.

If children's misdeeds are discovered then they feel that it is right and proper that punishment should follow; so, in stories when the villain is unmasked, they expect and demand that a terrible fate shall befall him and believe wholeheartedly in 'an eye for an eye and a tooth for a tooth'.

They also rejoice when the cunning and trickery of an evil-doer is discovered, although such behaviour on the part of the hero meets with definite approval. By seven, many children are becoming more objective in their judgments, better able to evaluate behaviour and the motives that lie behind a particular act and not so much influenced by the resultant damage. But it still depends to some extent on the actual situation and the intelligence and maturity of the child and more than one type of moral judgment can exist side by side.

Just because children are at the stage when they are still acquiring standards and values and sorting out their ideas of right and wrong, their stories need to show fairly clearly that goodness does, in fact, triumph over evil. Many of the old folk and fairy tales provide simple, clear-cut patterns, where wrong-doing is punished and goodness justified, though the fact that goodness is often its own reward is a truth that children only gradually begin to understand. Paul Hazard, in *Books, Children and Men*, puts this in an unforgettable way when he says:

> I like books that contain a profound morality ... that set in action truths worthy of lasting for ever and of inspiring one's whole inner life; those demonstrating that an unselfish and faithful love always ends by finding its own reward, be it only in oneself; – how ugly and low are envy, jealousy and greed; how people who utter only slander and lies end by coughing up vipers and toads whenever they speak. In short, I like books that have the integrity to perpetuate their own faith in truth and justice.

It is not always easy to know beforehand quite what is going to frighten young children either in stories or pictures. Sometimes a seemingly innocuous tale or illustration will upset one child yet be enjoyed by others. Probably the child who is frightened would have been left unaffected if he had not already been in the throes of an emotional conflict which in some way has become linked with the tale and its pictures. The adult cannot always foresee these difficulties, particularly as the reverse can also be true, when a really lurid and alarming picture story book leaves children quite unmoved. Occasionally one can explain to a child a frightening picture or story which has been misunderstood. Sometimes the children themselves will play out their fears, just as they often do about their visits to the doctor or dentist or other alarming experiences, and find relief and comfort in so doing.

Under five is not really the time for stories about fairies, ogres, witches, goblins and the like. One needs to be quite sure of solid things before meeting the magic of unreality and the young child's fanciful tales should not include the supernatural.

There are, of course, fantastic stories which, to children, seem perfectly natural, even though adults might think them akin to magic. The small child, for example, like his primitive forebears, tends to believe that inanimate objects have a life of their own. He would not be surprised if his teddy bear, like Pooh, suddenly spoke to him, or his engine ran away down the hill with a will of its own. Therefore, it is natural in stories about animals who behave like human beings, that they should talk, wear clothes, go to work and be endowed with feelings like himself. It is quite natural, to the child, for fire engines, steam rollers, trains or buses to hold interesting conversations. They are, after all, solid, everyday things with their roots in reality and yet, if they decide, suddenly, to burst into speech – why shouldn't they! There is no need to be surprised. It is creatures that are purely phantoms of the imagination which as yet the under five is not really ready for.

Stories in which animals or machines are captured, tamed or managed by the child – dominated by him or their roles taken over, have a very strong appeal, both to the under five and the five to eight-year-old. Symbolically they can represent the parents, and either the child feels himself stronger than they are and leads and commands the situation, or he is himself, in fantasy, the father or the mother figure and everyone must obey him. In Louise Fatio's story *The Happy Lion*, it is the little boy who is able to capture this fierce, father figure of a lion who terrifies the whole village. Then the lion turns out to be kind and gentle and so the child is reassured, as it were, of the fundamental goodness of fathers, even though they appear sometimes so strong and angry.

The same type of theme is repeated in Hardie Gramatsky's *Little Toot*, where a tiny tug boat with whom the child can also identify himself becomes the hero of the tale, outmanoeuvring all the big father boats. Stories of the weak and the small out-witting the strong and the mighty, or taking their place and succeeding where they have failed, are such well-known themes in myths, fairy stories, simple children's tales and those for adults, that we tend to overlook the deeper meaning which lies behind them.

In some stories, even parents harmlessly disappear, or are left out of the story altogether, and here the unconscious wish of the child to

21

rid himself of those frustrating adults who always prevent him from doing and having everything he wants, finds safe and happy fulfilment.

This is a favourite theme in stories for older children when, alone and unaided, they unmask spies, catch burglars and perform brave and heroic deeds unfettered by adult interference and stupidity. Round about five, many children – though not by any means all – will have come to terms with some of the problems that were so insistent at the preschool stage. They will feel more at home in the world, more secure and poised, surer of their place in the family and the role they themselves must play. Thus they are able to enjoy more exciting stories without quite so much anxiety, or feeling quite so deeply and personally involved.

One stage of development slowly merges into the next, well-loved stories and picture books will still be enjoyed and new ones will not be so very different in content, for many of the same themes will occur. Stories can be longer, however, and more complex and continued from one day to the next if they are being read or told to the children – provided each incident is complete in itself. The fairy story and myth both come into their own now, for children with a surer hold on reality are ready and eager for the fantasy of magic. About seven and a half to eight, though, there is no arbitrary line – there does develop a slight divergence of taste between boys and girls. Boys revel in adventure of all kinds and tend to think fairies, as such, babyish. Girls, on the other hand, tend to go on liking fairies for much longer; they also enjoy homely, family stories more than boys. Magic still thrills the male sex, and there are plenty of tales about knights, heroes, witches, giants and strange animals and machines which are full of exciting incidents.

Round about six, some children do seem to go through a slightly more awkward period. Second dentition can be disturbing – even with a tenpence under your pillow for the tooth that is about to come out or has already done so; and Gesell in *The Child from Five to Ten* points out that six-year-old children often have nightmares and are quarrelsome and contrary.

At this stage, too, new fears emerge or there is an upsurge of the old ones. Bears under the bed, lions lurking behind dressing gowns hanging on doors, or clothes draped over chairs, can make bedtime rather an alarming affair. It is perhaps wise, therefore, to avoid very exciting or frightening stories just when children are settling down to sleep. In any case, the dark is never light enough for many of us.

These fears are not necessarily really related to the animals mentioned but are generally linked with a child's feelings about his parents, which he gradually works through for himself in the secure and happy home.

At a slightly older age (about eight or over), though children vary in their needs and interests, some girls become passionately devoted to horses; horse stories, horse pictures, horse books completely absorb them and their one ambition appears to be either to possess a pony or work in a riding school. Here the horse probably stands as a sex symbol and as a girl develops and new contacts and wishes take up her time and energy, the horse loses his sexual appeal and takes a more normal and ordinary place in her life.

Many of the so-called 'classics of childhood' such, for example, as *Alice in Wonderland*, *The Wind in the Willows*, *The Secret Garden* and *Black Beauty*, are probably better left until children are about eight, though this, of course, will depend on the individual. Many children, too, may need these stories read aloud, finding them too long to tackle on their own even at the junior stage.

The giving and receiving of food is often synonymous to the child with the giving and receiving of love. So, stories where good things to eat are provided and enjoyed, provoke warm feelings of affection and pleasure. How small boys and girls delight in the number of pancakes *Little Black Sambo* eats, and how sad the older child feels when hearing Hans Andersen's tale of 'The Little Match Girl' who saw in fantasy in the light of her match, the glorious feast of food she so longed for, only to see it vanish when her match went out. The warm security of home in stories about loving and happy families, even if sad things do sometimes happen, remind children of the significance of home and perhaps help the child deprived of a normal home life to share by proxy in experiences that life is denying him.

There are all sorts of individual problems that a story, even for quite young children, can put into words, providing a simple plot and a solution which may help towards a better understanding. The new baby, being a twin, getting lost, going away from home, being ill, starting school, even death itself told in a dramatic tale with sympathy and understanding may help a child, through identification, to understand such experiences a little better so that if they do happen to him, he will at least have met them and shared them imaginatively with the characters in the stories.

One would take for granted that in tales told to children there should never be any implied suggestion that children or adults from a different country, of a different colour or appearance, whose ideas, traditions, and patterns of life are new and strange, are in any way inferior. This does not appear to happen in stories for young children, though some adults see an unpleasing caricature in *The Story of Little Black Sambo*. This I do not feel is so; Sambo is dearly loved by children who think of him as someone like themselves and he is so much a part of their early picture book heritage one could not imagine growing up without him.

Stories for older children, either by subtle implication, or more blatantly, do sometimes imply that coloured people are sly, underhand and untrustworthy while those with white skins are brave, honest and reliable. Such stories should be avoided.

We do not want children to feel that we are continually ramming home a moral: that is not the reason for a story's existence. It lives in its own right because, even at a child's level, it is a window onto the world to which children can respond actively, passively or imaginatively, on their own terms and in their own way. But a sense of values, a feeling for beauty and an integrity towards those aspects of life with which it deals should be implicit in the good story.

Through stories children can share at a simple level in fundamental human experiences and emotions. They can project their own bad behaviour, their feelings of jealousy, fear, insecurity, envy and hate on to the appropriate characters in the stories they hear and thus understand and come to terms more easily with reality. Nor should we deny young children the right to feel grief and pain, simple though it may be. To share the unhappiness of others in stories is to identify oneself with the sorrows of mankind. Children become aware of the universality of human emotion, of loss, misunderstanding, disappointment, disillusionment and heartache. We sometimes forget the relief of tears even for the young, and when we weep in a story for the unhappiness of the characters we can weep for all our own sorrows and losses for the times, perhaps, when we have longed to cry but could not, or when, if we were children, we were told to be brave and so fought back our tears, – now at last unashamedly we can cry for as many reasons as we wish.

One of the greatest assets of simple folk tales and nursery rhymes is that at the imaginative level they can introduce young children to the 'very culture of the feelings'.[1] Here, tragic, violent and frightening things do happen in fantasy, and all sorts of sad and aggressive events occur. Babies fall out of cradles, little pigs are eaten by wolves, boys are whipped, old men thrown downstairs, kittens lost, cock-robins killed. Yet, in the form in which young children hear them they clearly recognize them as belonging to the world of make-believe. In fantasy they accept and incorporate them into the very texture of their lives and so some of the tragedy, terror and compassion of the world has become theirs for now and all time.

[1] John Stuart Mill speaking of Wordsworth's poetry.

4

The Fantasy Tale

Tell me where is fancy bred,
Or in the heart, or in the head,
How begot, how nourished.
William Shakespeare

The enrichment of the imagination which grows and develops in so many ways in childhood, through play in all its aspects, through growing familiarity with the real world seen through the spontaneous wonder that is one of childhood's most enchanting qualities, is quickened and fed by picture books, stories and poetry, particularly perhaps by those rich in imaginative material.

The Concise Oxford Dictionary defines imagination as 'the process, the faculty or the result of forming representations of things not actually present'. The word fantasy comes from the Greek and if it is translated literally means 'a making visible'. Thus fantasy makes visible to the inward eye concepts that the creative imagination has given birth to.

What is imagined can only be built out of what has first been discovered in the real world, coloured by experience and enriched and intensified by feeling. E. M. Forster, in *Aspects of the Novel*, says, 'What does fantasy ask of us? It asks us to pay something extra.' Is this extra a sixth sense, the 'willing suspension of disbelief', the ability to cross the narrow bridge between sense and nonsense, fact and fancy, or the sudden discovery in ourselves of unconscious memories and dreams we had forgotten we possessed?

Children are singularly at home in the world of fantasy where they can deal with experiences and situations in their own way, taking over the roles they themselves wish to play, imitating the grown-up world yet discarding the rules and regulations invented by adults. In imagination they can hitch their wagons to stars or

26

ploughshares and, like Alice, pass through the mirror of their secret wishes.

To the very young child everything around him is new and exciting and he does not know what to expect of even the most mundane of subjects. He is, therefore, not ready for stories of supernatural magic; the real world is overflowing with fantastic happenings which are infinitely satisfying and enough for his present needs.

Round about five, however, when children have more or less sorted out for themselves the main differences between the world of reality and fantasy they are ready, and eager for the enrichment that the fairy story, folk tale or simple myth can provide. In spite of the fact that these tales deal with events that one might suppose the modern child, with his interest in jet planes, racing cars and excursions to the moon, would scorn and despise, this is not so; children enjoy them tremendously and ask for them again and again, making such remarks as, 'I didn't want it to end, ever', 'I loved the bit when I felt scared', 'I kept wondering and wondering what was going to happen next', 'Do, do tell it again'.

Now these old tales belong to the early life of mankind and their roots go down into the remote past, a past which we all possess within us, even though we may be unaware of it. Deep within us all are intense primitive impulses of love, hate and aggression bound up in our very early years with our feelings about our parents and our brothers and sisters. These feelings lie so deep within us, forgotten and repressed, that we are unaware of their existence, yet they exert an unconscious influence on our behaviour. The old tales are deeply concerned with these early fantasies, feelings, needs and motives of behaviour, which they incorporate for us in story form. All humankind shares these fantasies; they are universal and that is why one finds the same kinds of tales all the world over.

The idea that was once current that travellers took these stories from country to country in their wanderings and for that reason one found the same themes constantly appearing in widely different parts of the world, no doubt has a grain of truth in it, but the similarity of these basic themes lies rooted in the nature of man himself. They are written too, in the language of symbolism, a universal language that speaks to us all at an unconscious level and that we can all understand. A very important human need is security; to feel safely protected and provided for; for the world must have seemed a cruel and hostile place to human beings, full of things they could neither understand nor explain. It still does. So, warm fires with their leaping flames, the bright and kindly sun, luxuriant flowers and fruit, wonderful feasts with food and drink in abundance for all, rich and costly clothes, sparkling jewels and exquisite palaces, which are so much a part of the fairy tale, were man's symbols of security.

One can well understand primitive feelings about the universe for, like the young child, man endowed inanimate objects with feelings and desires like himself. The sun, moon and stars, wind and water, rivers and mountains, thunder and lightning, all must have seemed alive to him, about to vent anger and hate in destruction, storm and flood, or to be benign and gentle, kindly with warmth, generous with growing life. It is not surprising, therefore, to have countless stories and myths where the elements take on human form and behave in a human way, when a god rises from the sea or drives the chariots of the sun across the sky.

Man, too, felt a deep kinship with animals and imagined that they also possessed feelings like himself. In the old tales animals often took on human form and men and women were mysteriously changed into bears, leopards, deer, swans or fish. In the early versions of the Cinderella cycle of stories the fairy godmother, so prominent now and who appears in Perrault's version, was absent. It was an animal who came to Cinderella and helped her, often her real mother in disguise. There are innumerable tales where animals, birds or fish help the hero or heroine overcome some difficulty or complete some lengthy task.

Animals serve the useful purpose of symbolising for children their parents or some other heroic or frightening character, and they can be both loved and hated, rejected and accepted.

If a human sacrifice was needed an animal could be substituted or eaten and his strength and cunning incorporated by his slayers with no feelings of guilt which the death of a person might involve. There were, of course, certain taboos connected with certain animals and tribes, and the relationship between the two was exceedingly complex. The ancient Christian Church took over many of the old pagan customs, festivals, traditions, and super-stitions, and used them (still does use them) for her own needs and purposes. The communion service enables those who partake of it to feel that symbolically they are receiving the body and blood of Christ, incorporating within themselves His strength and wisdom.

The family has always been a place, not only where there are love, security, self-sacrifice and compassion, but also where hatred, jealousy, rivalry, possessiveness and envy flourish. There is hatred of paternal and maternal authority; the desire all children have to become independent and to rid themselves in fantasy of those frustrating adults whom they both love and hate, fear and admire, and who prevent them from doing and having exactly what they want. There is the feeling of the parents too, who see in their growing children not only exacting burdens but also possible rivals, so they must be pushed out, lost or destroyed. There is the envy and jealousy among children in the family from the young child's first angry manifestations when a new baby arrives, to the intensely hostile impulses that children often experience towards each other, even in the best brought up families.

There is the age-old desire of a boy for the exclusive love and possession of his mother, and the daughter for her father, exempli-fied in the well-known Oedipus myth[1] – an ever recurring theme in real life and in modern plays and novels.

Mothers and daughters, fathers and sons, get rid of each other in devious ways in fairy tales; and sometimes, to make a story more acceptable and less harrowing, it is a step-mother or father, or parents who are wicked and cruel, who is destroyed in some horrible disaster. Fathers send their sons out on dangerous adventures; mothers suggest that their daughters find some strange food; both

---

[1] 'It was foretold in the Oedipus myth that King Laius of Thebes and his wife Jocasta would have a son who would slay his father and marry his mother. To escape this fate when Oedipus was born, he was given to a shepherd to abandon but is saved and is brought up by the King of Corinth and believes himself to be his son. He meets his father whom he unknowingly kills in an argument. In his wanderings, he finally reaches Thebes where he solves the riddle of the Sphinx and is given his widowed mother's hand in marriage as a reward. When he eventually discovers what he has unwittingly done, committed both patricide and incest, he blinds himself, and Jocasta commits suicide.' – From Eric Fromm, *The Forgotten Language*, Gollancz 1952.

missions are such that the children are not expected to return alive. Kings imprison their daughters in castles or towers in order to prevent them marrying, or set their respective suitors impossible tasks. This is a way of trying to possess their daughters and keep both them and their kingdoms for themselves. Children are lost like 'The Babes in the Wood' or 'Hansel and Gretel'.

Sometimes children take the place of the appropriate parent as in the story of 'Baba Yaga and the Little Girl with the Kind Heart';[1] for not only are there a cruel step-mother and several animals who help the little girl, but when the step-mother dies horribly the child returns to look after her father and live with him happily ever after.

Jealousy and rivalry between siblings is a favourite topic in fairy tales and younger brothers and sisters are put upon and ill-treated by older members of the family. In the end it is generally the youngest who wins the prize or reaps the reward, for the downfall of the mighty and the triumph of the small and the weak is a dearly loved theme.

In the Bible story of Joseph and his brethren, one sees the lengths to which other members of a family will go in order to rid themselves of a hated rival. Heroes and heroines are an important element in stories for children who need people that they can admire and copy; in some cases these figures symbolize the ideal parents or the mates that all children seek. It is perhaps easiest to understand the origin of witches, ghosts, demons, devils, evil spirits and the like, if one considers them in terms of the bad, cruel and hateful things which originally the young child projected outside himself on to his all-powerful parents. Gradually, however, these bad things become separated from the original parental figures and take on other forms. Under cover of the mechanism known as 'projection' whereby all the wickedness is in others, not in ourselves, human beings have taken part in acts of the greatest cruelty.

Thus the sadistic horror of many of the old tales have their counterpart both in the past and the present. As Susan Isaacs points out in *Social Development in Young Children*, 'human history sets forth an unending tale of burning, maiming, killing, torturing, imprisonment and all the resources of human ingenuity in devising cruel

[1] Arthur Ransome, *Old Peter's Russian Tales*, Nelson.

revenge under the pressure of this mechanism. We have only to turn back the clock to 1939 and the concentration camps to see how thin is the dividing line between primitive barbarism and civilization.

Evil is personified for children in the characters of witches, demons, etc., and when in Hans Andersen's tale of 'The Tinder Box' the soldier cuts off the head of the old witch who, in actual fact, had done nothing wrong, the children are delighted.

It must not be forgotten that children (and adults) have kind and loving feelings too, and fantasies are projected in childhood on to kind and ideally good parents who, in their turn represent handsome princes, good fairies, angels, sympathetic godmothers and the like.

All these family themes appear in the old tales and because they are removed from children's real lives and appear as magic, boys and girls do not feel guilty when they identify themselves with the characters in the stories and the emotions they experience.

If life was frightening to human beings, death must have been equally so and it haunted the mind of primitive man just as it haunts us today. The ancient Egyptians were so concerned with death that they built their whole civilization round it. It has been said that in the unconsciousness of each one of us we ourselves are immortal, unconsciously we cannot conceive our own death – and young children cannot believe they will ever die. Others may die, but not them; death is the father and mother of all fears. There is a great deal of mystery and magic associated with death. It is concerned with the unhappiness of separation and often seems to be aggression at its most final. It is associated too, with feelings of guilt, and the need for acts of reparation or even retaliation. Many primitive people did not believe that death was due to old age or disease but that some enemy had made aggressive and hostile magic which brought about the victim's end. Hence all the strange rites, tales, and superstitions of the witch doctors aimed, not at the illness, but at the evil spirits which had entered the victim.

One often gets references in myths and fairy stories to death by being swallowed or drowned, the connection here being, an identification of a future life with the pre-natal life in the womb, a place often envisaged as one of complete security. Jonah was swallowed by a whale and there are numerous fairy tales and myths where the

31

hero finds himself in the belly of some animal or fish where he is temporarily protected. There is also a close link between what is called 'fairy land', and the world where the dead dwell, for many so-called fairies were thought of as spirits of the departed.

The relationship between earth and heaven is sometimes symbolized by a tree or other growing thing as in 'Jack and the Beanstalk', or with a ladder, as in the biblical myth of 'Jacob's Ladder'.

Perhaps from the moment when the baby's first aggressive and piteous cries appeared as mysterious acts of power generally having the desired effect, the appearance of love or food, language acquired a certain magical quality. Words became strong and powerful things to be used in all sorts of ways as spells, incantations, charms, curses, blessings etc. – 'Open Sesame', 'Abracadabra' and numerous phrases of this kind which gave people power over others.

An individual's spoken name had this magical quality about it, and sometimes had to be altered, or a nickname substituted so that one's enemy would not have the power to harm one through knowledge of one's real name. The stories of 'Tom Tit Tot' and 'Rumpelstiltskin' are tales where the knowledge of an individual's proper name acted as a magic spell bringing misfortune in its wake.

Christenings or the ceremonies associated with naming a child were particularly dangerous events and wicked witches or demons cast their cruel spells, or evil spirits took the opportunity of harming a child at this time. The story of 'The Sleeping Beauty' shows how easy it was to offend a witch, who then cast her cruel spells on an innocent child.

People may first have given objects names in order that they might control them. One gets the same idea of the magic of words in the biblical creation myth:

> And the earth was without form and void; and darkness was upon the face of the deep, and the spirit of God moved upon the face of the waters. And God said, 'Let there be light', and there was light.

In the beginning the old tales were all told by word of mouth and so belonged to everyone; nor were they conceived for the delight of children, for boys and girls were merely thought of as miniature adults. The finished stories that gradually emerged were the results of centuries of being told and retold and handed down from one generation to another. In the process they became not only highly polished, often acquiring a simple impressiveness, but they often acquired too, the distortions that made them more acceptable. Descriptions in the old tales were always kept to a minimum for it was the drama that mattered, so anything that a listener could imagine for himself was left out. There were also conventional beginnings and endings – 'Once upon a time', 'They lived happily ever after' and so on – to save time and help in the remembering of a tale. Although many of these old stories possess a cruel and some-times horrifying quality, they did at least put the stamp of approval upon certain simple values; even though they often appealed to what was not really the best, it was generally to something better rather than something still worse.

Adult human beings in the early days were like children still in the process of developing a moral code. Like children, too, the penalties they demanded for wrong-doing were often too terrible to contemplate. On the other hand they had a certain primitive justice; if wrong-doing was violently punished, virtue was re-warded. Many of the old tales did in fact teach a certain simple kindness, modesty and courage, showing that though the heavens fall, good will eventually triumph over evil. In speaking of these old tales, R. Money-Kyrle, in *Superstition and Society*, says:

> To have a strong and universal appeal, a story must satisfy at least three conditions. It must represent some fundamental unconscious fantasy which is common to the greater part of mankind in every age and culture. It must be distorted suf-ficiently to satisfy conscious standards, yet it must be clear enough to be immediately intelligible to the unconscious. And it must have sufficient secondary elaboration to be free from the absurdities and irrationalities which would otherwise offend the conscious mind.

It is of course very difficult to differentiate between myths, folk tales and fairy stories. Folk tales are perhaps less sophisticated, simpler in form and linked with the more ordinary life of the common people. The myth, as Eric Fromm suggests,[1] 'offers a story

[1] *The Forgotten Language*, Gollancz.

occurring in space and time which expresses in symbolic language religious and philosophical ideas', however crude, primitive, cruel and aggressive these ideas often appear to us today. The fairy story dealt with supernatural beings of all kinds who could take on human form, help or harm human beings and have their links with the dead in fairy land. Yet all these types of tale tend to overlap in content and meaning, and contain many elements in common. They embody our efforts to explain ourselves and the world in which we live. They acted in the past as a codifying force, cementing human beings together, showing them their need of each other and by their suggestions of certain acceptable forms of behaviour – however crude they seem to us now – providing a social conscience; all bound up in exciting and dramatic tales which could be remembered long after the storyteller had vanished.

What of modern fantasy tales. Obviously they must speak to children in much the same way as the old tales, reflecting their inner fantasies and providing them with acceptable solutions through identification of their problems. Often they show, symbolically, the human struggle between the forces of good and evil, and much the same sort of evil as the old tales described – 'Envy, hatred, malice and all uncharitableness' as in C. S. Lewis's Narnia stories. Sometimes they are concerned with longings and aspirations expressed in a language and a form that children can understand, or with human kinship with the animals as in Hugh Lofting's Dr Dolittle stories or Kipling's *The Jungle Books.*

Many modern fantasy tales can be interpreted at more than one level for they contain hidden truths, allegories and philosophical ideas, while there is also the sheer magic of fantasy, with all its delight, excitement, originality of theme and the vividness of its characterization.

Many present day stories stress the value of compassion, understanding, kindness and love with far less emphasis on cruelty, punishment and revenge. So they are less crude and primitive, partly because humans have developed a more sensitive conscience, but also because these stories are written especially for children and the old tales were created for everyone. The modern fantasy story, however, will lose its appeal if it does not keep in touch with children's inner conflicts and needs, remembering that imaginative material is the basis of all creative work.

Story-telling Time with the Six- and Seven-year-olds[1]

The story of 'The Tinder Box' by Hans Andersen was thoroughly enjoyed by the children. The tale is the familiar one of the soldier who is told by an old witch where to find a wonderful treasure guarded by three magic dogs, the old witch's only request being a tinder box that the soldier would find. All the money the soldier discovers makes him rich and after many adventures he succeeds in marrying a beautiful princess who is confined in a copper tower: all this, of course, with the help of the magic tinder box and the magic dogs. There was a lot of discussion by the children about witches, for the soldier had cut off the old woman's head when he had found the treasure and had kept for himself the tinder box she had asked for.

To the children the old witch was the personification of evil, thus, through unconscious identification they were able to work through their feelings of fear in relation to their mother for the witch represented the bad, denying frustrating side of her personality and their feelings of hate towards her. 'Witches should be got dead before any more trouble happens'; 'Witches are horrible with beastly horrid faces, long clawey nails and they have a thick lip hanging down. I'm afraid of witches – they run after you'; 'Witches are mean and ugly with huge teeth' were some of the remarks the children made. Only one child felt that the witch had been treated unjustly.

The king and queen in the story had heard the prophecy that their daughter would marry a common soldier, hence her imprisonment in the copper tower. By magic, the poor soldier entices her away but when he is discovered, he is told he will be hanged.

This part of the story intrigued the children who appeared quite familiar with the process of hanging.

'People should be hanged if they do something really bad like stealing a crumb from a king and I'd put them in a dungeon and keep them there the rest of their lives with no food except water, maybe sometimes a hard crust of bread, and I'd make it very stale',

---

[1] This section is based on an unpublished thesis by Mrs Sara Corrin and the author is grateful to her for her permission to use it.

a $6\frac{1}{2}$-year-old said. 'I think murdering about worse than stealing because they might murder someone very important like the Lord Mayor', was another remark. A little girl who sometimes acted in children's films spoke very dramatically: 'I wouldn't like to see hanging. I know what it's like to be hanged because I saw *Wagon Train*. No, I wouldn't like anyone to be hanged – I'd find another punishment.' One boy was very curious about hanging: 'I liked it when he was going to be hanged. I'd like to see somebody hanged: not because I don't like them, but I'd like to see the rope being pulled. Really I'd like to see a dummy.'

When the soldier succeeded, with the help of the magic dogs and the witch's tinder box, in marrying the princess, there was great rejoicing and the fact that the king and queen were torn to bits by the magic dogs pleased every one. 'Serve them right' was the general feeling.

'The Twelve Dancing Princesses' by the Brothers Grimm was very popular. 'I love it so much that I don't want to stop hearing it', said a six-year-old. This story tells of twelve princesses who wore their shoes out dancing every night. The king offered the hand of one of his daughters in marriage to the man who could discover where they went. A poor soldier with an invisible cloak outwits the princesses, discovers their nightly visits and marries the youngest. The children soon realise that it is generally the youngest who is the successful one.

At a point of suspense in the story, a $6\frac{1}{2}$-year-old burst out, 'I wonder which one he'll have – I bet it will be the youngest'. The child next to her said, 'Yes, it's nearly always the youngest'. All the children remembered the word 'invisible' in relation to the soldier's cloak.

They did not turn a hair when they heard of the suitors who had tried to solve the problem of the dancing princesses, had failed and had had their heads cut off. It was only when the poor soldier appeared that there was any feeling of emotional involvement. 'I loved the bit when they danced and danced and danced till their shoes were full of holes 'cos I knew the soldier would find out', said a six-year-old almost hugging himself with satisfaction. The story met with universal approval.

'Rumpelstiltskin' is a story that is linked with the magic of names and is a familiar and well-loved one.

A miller boasted that his daughter could spin yarn into gold thread. The king heard of this and demanded that the girl demonstrate her skill, and win his son's hand in marriage or be beheaded if she failed. A little dwarf heard her weeping and promised to help her, provided she gave him, first a necklace, then a bracelet and finally her baby when she had one. As the girl succeeded in her task, she marries the prince and when the king dies she becomes queen. Eventually she has a beautiful baby. Then the little dwarf appears to demand the child. He says, however, that he will relinquish his claim if the queen can guess his name. She succeeds of course. The dwarf is furiously angry, stamps his foot with rage and disappears through the floor for ever.

The children all thought the miller 'jolly foolish' for boasting and lying about his daughter's accomplishments. Although the dwarf helped the miller's daughter, he got no sympathy from the children. 'I hate him; he's little, he's a dwarf. I hate dwarfs – they're small and silly.' 'He's horrid. He's a nut case because he's ugly and horrid.' 'He's mean to ask for such a promise', were some of the comments.

One boy with a young baby in his family revealed his unconscious jealousy when he said: 'Well, it's not so terrible if the queen did give him the baby – she could always get another one.' The children laughed delightedly, probably feeling a relief from tension, when the queen who had discovered the dwarf's name, pretended she didn't know it and guessed all sorts of wrong ones first. They revelled in the rather frightening aspects of the story. 'I like to be frightened', said one child. 'I always like creepy things; this is a creepy story in an exciting sort of way.' The children suggested all sorts of wonderful names themselves when they retold the tale.

One child said, 'Is your name Pox? Is your name Bisteg? Is your name Bagshole? Is your name Fingle?' When she came to the tenth try she said, 'Is your name Rumpelstiltskin and he shrieked and he stamped his foot terribly loud because he was so angry. She guessed and he stamped his foot right through the floor and disappeared for ever.'

5

Poetry and Young Children

A living poem is one that stays alive because it is rooted in mortal things and deathless emotions. It is felt first and thought out afterwards. It begins. 'Frost once wrote in a letter'. With a lump in the throat. A homesickness or a love sickness. It is a reaching out towards expression; an effort to find fulfilment. A complete poem is one where an emotion has found its thought, and the thought has found the words.

Robert Frost

In his essay 'A boy and his books',[1] George Sampson, speaking of poetry, says 'I wonder when you made your first acquaintance with poets? Was a love of poetry part of your nature growing unnoticed with your growth till at last it became manifest? Or did there come a moment when words in a certain order suddenly gave you a strange thrill?'

Looking back to my own childhood, some poetry seems to have been a part of my life as long as I can remember and thinking of the images that are brought to my mind when I hear them now. I realize that many of them are the very ones that I had as a child. So one slips back in time and place, and pictures that are lovely and familiar – the pictures of childhood – appear before one's eyes.

One day I remember I discovered that an experience that had delighted me was put into just the right words, for I heard Robert Louis Stevenson's poem 'The Swing' at the very moment when I had acquired one myself. How I revelled in this shared experience and how wonderful it seemed to me that someone who had never known me, yet understood exactly how I felt:

> How do you like to go up in a swing,
> Up in the air so blue?
> Oh, I do think it the pleasantest thing

---

[1] *Seven Essays*, CUP.

Ever a child can do!

Up in the air and over the wall
Till I can see so wide,
Rivers and trees and cattle and all
Over the country side.

Not only were the feelings just right – I, too, could see almost exactly what Robert Louis Stevenson described. There, before my eyes was a wide expanse of country with little square fields dotted with animals; there were trees and even a river. What could be more perfect than that!

Then there was the fascination in gradually discovering the way different people saw and felt about the same thing. My mother read me what I always felt was a sad and lovely poem about the moon:

'Lady Moon, Lady Moon,
Where are you roving?'
'Over the sea.'
'Lady Moon, Lady Moon,
Whom are you loving?'
'All that love me.' [1]

And as I watched the moon in the night sky I had a vivid image of a stately, omnipotent individual looking sorrowfully, yet serenely down on me, a small, insignificant little girl.

She also read me, *Wynken, Blynken and Nod* [2], where quite a different moon appeared – a jovial and smiling one. Then there was Robert Louis Stevenson's moon who had a face 'like the clock in the hall' and the one the cow jumped over; in fact there were hundreds of them. Thus I found I possessed not one moon but many; all were different and all exciting and new in their own special way and my looking and feeling were immeasurably enriched by hearing so many moon poems.

If poetry was something that charmed and excited me, it can do the same for other young children – charm and excite them too, provided it is given to them with wisdom and understanding. Children are fascinated by words from the moment they begin to realize that everything has a name. They invent their own and very

---

[1] 'Lady Moon', by Lord Houghton.   [2] By Eugene Field.

soon they discover that words are things that can be played with and are strong and powerful and bring the world running to their side. They can be chanted, shouted and sung; collected like flowers and used with love and hate. Soon children discover that they have a rhythm of their own and can be linked with actions;

> 'I'm running up the stairs,
>
> I'm running up the stairs,
>
> Up, down, up, down,
>
> I'm running up the stairs,'

chanted four-year-old Mark, who had suddenly discovered that his words could be made to fit the rhythm of his moving feet.

> Splash I go
>
> Splosh, splosh,
>
> Then I go splash again,

sang Nora to a funny little tune of her own as she played with the water in the basin. Words are the basic material from which all poetry is formed.

'Poetry', says Shelley, 'turns all things to loveliness.' Coleridge defined poetry as the 'best words in the best order', and children, too, soon become aware of the importance of their order and arrangement. We probably owe the very survival of many old rhymes to the fact that children adore to hear the things they love over and over again in exactly the same words. So, down the centuries has gone the cry, 'Say it again, just the same'.

Although most nursery rhymes were not originally written for children and are fragments of ancient ballads, remnants of old rituals, customs, street cries, proverbs, political satires, riddles, prayers and so on, they are steeped in the vigour, vitality and humanity of ordinary folk, built up on simple human experiences. One can imagine children listening to them, absorbing even if not understanding them, and demanding their constant repetition, so making them a part of their everyday lives, remembered for ever.

The very young love sound, speed and action in the things they hear and, fortunately, early poetry is often bound up with real things to do, so that small babies can join in the fun and there are finger plays and rhymes to go with all sorts of simple occasions. How many millions of children have been bathed and dried to the words, 'This little pig went to market', or kept quiet and amused to the refrain, 'Pat a cake, pat a cake, baker's man'. There is often the delight of a nonsense line that can be lisped or shouted:

> Diddlety diddlety dumpty
> The cat ran up the plum tree;
> Half a crown to fetch her down
> Diddlety diddlety dumpty.

Or small boys and girls can be dandled on the knee to:

> Leg over, leg over,
> As the dog went to Dover
> When he came to the stile
> Jump! he went over.

In fact, nursery rhymes are all-embracing, and moods, feelings and experience of all kinds are here for the taking.

The many devices used by the poet to get the effect he wants mean nothing to children for they are unaware of the part played by figurative language in their enjoyment of a poem. Yet, these uncommon and out of the ordinary methods of expression gradually become a part of the texture of their listening. When the poet, for example, compares things, setting them side by side so that one brightens and illuminates the other, they accept the rightness of it without question; it could not be done in any other way:

> My bed is like a little boat
> Nurse tucks me in when I embark
> She girds me in my sailor's coat
> And starts me in the dark.[1]
>
> Twinkle, twinkle little star
> How I wonder what you are.
> Up above the world so high
> Like a diamond in the sky.[2]

They do not know what a simile is, but for all that they have heard them and enjoyed them.

When Alison, playing in the garden, picked a bunch of dandelions and called them 'orange suns' she did not know she was using the language of the metaphor but she was suddenly transfixed

---

[1] Robert Louis Stevenson, 'My Bed is a Boat' in *A Child's Garden of Verse*.
[2] By Jane and Ann Taylor.

by the wonder of the words she had used.

Children adore exaggeration – the hyperbole of the poet who says 'they were swifter than eagles, they were stronger than lions' excites them tremendously. They, on their part, may say, 'I'm as big as the world', or 'I can fly to the moon in a flash', and both poet and child understand what they mean.

Many words have originated by human beings trying to imitate natural sounds: water, wind, thunder and the noises of animals and birds and this is something that children do repeatedly when they themselves invent a word. Children's play when they are pretending to be trains, aeroplanes, bandits, pirates, or Red Indians is full of sounds which suggest words and words which suggest sounds, so there is nothing strange to them when poetry does the same thing. And just as the sounds that children make in their play help to create the atmosphere they need, so the sounds in poetry do the same thing.

The poet's imagination and the child's have in common – among other things – a spontaneous freshness and a sense of wonder and expectancy. 'To live in a nut shell and to count yourself the king of infinite space'[1] is, to them, well within the bounds of possibility. Young children's images are vivid and intense, built up on their perceptual experiences, and this applies to the poet also. Because of his peculiar genius, however, the poet is able to see things more clearly, more sensitively and with more awareness than most of us. His imagery is something which can give intense pleasure and satisfaction, both to children and to adults. The use he makes of words, their arrangement and rightness, conjures up the brightest and clearest of pictures. Suddenly, for the first time, we see some ordinary sight new born and re-created by the poet's touch. He has seized upon the very heart of an experience, coloured it with his own emotion and described it in words that are unforgettable.

It is not only visual images that the poet gives us: our response may be to sound when the traveller

> smote upon the door a second time;
> 'Is there anybody there?' he said.[2]

---

[1] Francis Thompson, *Shelley*.
[2] Walter de la Mare, *The Listener*.

to texture, the feel of snow, 'Silently sifting and veiling, road roof and railing',[1] or to heat and cold. Six-year-old Susan always used to fetch the blanket from her doll's bed and put it over her knees when she listened to the poem,

> All round the house is the jet-black night:
> It stares through the window-pane;
> It crawls in the corners, hiding from the light,
> And it moves with the moving flame.
>
> Now my little heart goes a-beating like a drum,
> With the breath of the Bogie in my hair;
> And all round the candle the crooked shadows come
> And go marching along up the stair.[2]

– because she said it made her feel cold and clammy.

So there is continued enrichment and stimulation of the imagination in a multitude of different ways. Imagination, perhaps more than any other quality, makes for insight and understanding into the feelings and thoughts of other human beings and is a quality that is vitally important to all of us.

To endow inanimate things with a life and personality of their own has always seemed perfectly natural to primitive people, children and poets. To personify something and give it human attributes therefore has an instinctive and universal appeal often used in poetry. It tends to make whatever is being described more real to us because it has taken on the form of a living creature rather than remaining an inanimate object. It has an instant appeal to children because it is a part of their own thinking. How intimate, for example, is a tide which behaves as we do –

> The tide in the river
> The tide in the river
> The tide in the river runs deep.
> I saw a shiver
> Pass over the river
> As the tide turned in its sleep.[3]

Deep in all of us is this feeling of kinship with the earth and

---

[1] Robert Bridges, 'London Snow'.

[2] Robert Louis Stevenson, 'Shadow March', in *A Child's Garden of Verse*.

[3] Eleanor Farjeon, *Silver Sand and Snow*.

everything that springs from it. How often we imagine that when we are carefree and happy the very earth itself becomes as sunny and gay as our mood, while the dripping rain and dark cloud is an echo of our own misery and depression.

In children's early years, poetry is often a part of their lives for most mothers spontaneously say or sing nursery rhymes to them. Then poetry seems to vanish altogether and no more is heard about it. Children meet it again at school and it may be with enjoyment and pleasure or it may be with boredom and apathy. If real poetry cannot help speaking to children in a very special way, surprising them with its richness, catching at their imaginations and perhaps epitomising an emotional experience for them in a way that nothing else can, then, it seems vital that poetry should be there, available, given to them freely, in a way they can accept and enjoy.

The adult should be able, therefore, to give children poetry of the right kind and at the right moment when they want it – as we try to give children other vital experiences just when they are most needed. This means that we should all have a store of remembered poetry and I mean real poetry, at our finger ends on which to draw, as well as books to help us. One does not want to drag in a line of verse or a poem at a time when children are obviously absorbed in something else, but there are moments when those of us who are with children can bring poetry into their every day lives in an exciting and personal way.

John, coming into Nursery School one morning had had his cap blown off by a blustering March breeze and he was just in the mood to hear:

> I saw you toss the kites on high,
> And blow the birds across the sky,
> And all around I heard you pass
> Like ladies' skirts across the grass.
> Oh wind a-blowing all day long,
> Oh wind that sings so loud a song.[1]

He listened with a gleam in his eye, 'It blew off my cap and it blew my mummy's dress', he said with a satisfied grin, and then he

---

[1] Robert Louis Stevenson, 'The Wind', in *A Child's Garden of Verse*.

44

rushed off into the garden calling out at the top of his voice, 'Wind, wind, noisy old wind'.

Judy, playing with the doll's dresser which had a little key to it listened entranced to 'I know a little cupboard with a teeny, tiny key'[1] and she went round the nursery chanting to herself, 'teeny, tiny key, teeny, tiny key', in her little sing-song voice.

Peter, aged seven, watching a butterfly alight on a flower heard:

> Down the air
> He falls.sunlazy debonair
> Upon a daisy.[2]

He opened his eyes very wide, crinkled his nose, and murmured quietly, 'fab' and that was all he needed to say – everyone knew what he meant.

Lullabies have a charm all their own and they can be said or sung to tired infants, and children themselves will repeat them in their play to their favourite dolls or teddy bears. The words and music of 'Hush-abye baby' have a gentle soothing quality and 'The old grey goose is dead', an American lullaby, with its haunting tune and words, introduces a child to death and disaster in a form that can be accepted and incorporated.

Boys and girls are fascinated by living and growing things, by the natural world around them and by the man-made environment of machines and buildings. To be able to enrich these experiences by words that fire the imagination as poetry can, is to give children treasure beyond price and there is unlimited treasure available. As the Opies have shown in *The Lore and Language of School Children*, boys and girls have a store of rhymes which can be used on all sorts of occasions and these rhymes grow and change as the need arises for material of topical interest. A refrain or verse that has a lilt or swing about it is as popular with the under fives as it is with the older children and when a group of three- and four-year-olds heard Edward Lear's verse:

> Calico Ban
> The little mice ran
> To be ready in time for tea,

[1] Walter de la Mare, 'The Cupboard', in *Peacock Pie*.
[2] S. Thomas Ansell, 'The Butterfly', in *The Countryman*.

Flippity flup,
They drank it all up
And danced in the cup –
But they never came back to me!
They never came back –
They never came back –
They never came back to me![1]

it proved quite irresistible. They chanted it and recited it to all and sundry and used it in all sorts of spontaneous play. Many of Edward Lear's poems are amongst those that make children laugh, perhaps because Lear himself wrote them for relaxation and fun as an antidote to his rather formal work as a scientific illustrator of birds and animals. The six- and seven-year-olds enjoy the limericks with their humorous drawings and their refreshingly amusing verse and the eccentric characters who do such peculiar things in them. In the longer poems: 'The Pobble Who Had No Toes', 'The Quangle Wangle's Hat', they are intrigued by the use of made up words as this is something they themselves adore doing.

Repetition in poetry, as in stories, is always satisfying. It appeals to children's sense of ritual. There is a magic in repeating a pattern of words more than once – a feeling of safety in a sudden return to a familiar refrain that everyone knows.

Poetry that contains a dramatic story always appeals to children and 'The Three Little Kittens Who Lost Their Mittens', 'John Gilpin' or parts of 'The Pied Piper of Hamelin' are enjoyed.

Obviously for both the under fives and the five- to seven-year-olds, a poem must not be too long and must swiftly and imaginatively seize the very heart of the experience which it is interpreting: an experience which the children can understand, described in language that holds them.

If an exciting story is unfolded verse by verse then children's attention can be held for longer. We, as adults, will choose the poetry young children hear, for they cannot browse through anthologies and poetry books and choose for themselves as the older boy and girl can. Nor, except very rarely, are they able to reread a poem for themselves through the medium of the pictures, as they can their

[1] 'Calico Pie', in *The Complete Nonsense of Edward Lear*, Faber.

favourite stories, for illustrated poetry books are few and far between. It is sometimes argued that because poetry makes its appeal through the medium of word images, pictures are out of place. Actually many children, and adults too, find it difficult to imagine things for themselves and words alone do not give them the visual images they need, they want something to start them off.

Collections of nursery rhymes are almost always illustrated and I should like to see a great many small picture poetry books for young children so that they could reread the poems through the illustrations as they can reread the stories they love in their ordinary picture story books. We all know how quickly a child learns a short tale by heart, and we often imagine a child can read when, in actual fact, he is – with the help of the pictures – recalling the written words that go with them because he has heard them so often. How much easier poetry is to remember with its rhythm, its beat and the sound and pattern of its word arrangement. Books of this kind, picture poetry books, would provide young children with a background of known verse that would last them all their lives.

The illustrations must of course be good, but there is no reason why they should spoil the poems, leaving too little for the children to imagine for themselves; this argument could apply to almost any picture book.

Good illustrations charm, delight and satisfy a child, and often stimulate his imagination. Decorations, such as appear in many anthologies, are often attractive but they are not enough, and colour, which appeals enormously to children, is hardly ever used in poetry books other than nursery rhymes.

The sizes of children's books tend to vary from the very large to the quite small. Poetry books should not be enormous tomes; older children can feel overwhelmed and discouraged at seeing so much to read, and younger children – because the pictures would tend to be disconnected, each one illustrating a separate poem – can also feel bewildered if too much is presented to them at once. We have a wonderful poetic heritage to offer our children, yet few of them grow up with either the desire or the ability to enjoy and accept it.

A question often asked by students, teachers and parents is: 'How can I judge a poem and know whether it is something which is worth reading to the children?' We all pick up magazines, bumper annuals, little volumes of verse and, alas, educational papers containing short, easy poems, and we wonder whether we can use them at the appropriate moment with the children. Sometimes these poems seem to fit the teacher's need very well. They can be linked with what the children are doing: nature, a story, or some aspect of their play. They are ready to hand and can be produced without effort. Generally, though not always, these little verses are without any literary merit. Why are they so poor and is there any criteria we can use in judging them?

In the first place these little verses are often pathetically trite, with nothing to stimulate a child's imagination. The language used is meagre and uninteresting but just because the words often appear to trip off the tongue easily, we are inclined to think that they suit a young child's limited understanding and experience.

Words fascinate children both for their sound and the way in which they are used; figurative language, the simile and metaphor, for example, which the genuine poet uses so skilfully to create his word images, can really thrill children. They do demand, however, that the similarity between the objects compared is one that, once the poet has revealed it to us, enchants and surprises by its vividness and truth. There are numerous examples to be found in second-rate verse where the figurative language used has no significance. When, for instance, Rose Fyleman suggests in her poem 'The Fairies' that these small creatures 'take a little star to make a fan' a simile is drawn which has no real meaning, for stars and fans have nothing whatsoever in common – and never will have. So the use of such language is something we can and should examine in the poetry we read to children as to its real quality and value. Poor verse, too, often does not ring true; the feelings expressed are shallow, sugary and sentimental, childish without being childlike.

Young children do not want highly intense and dramatic emotion concerned with adult problems but they do want emotion, on a scale that they can accept, that is completely genuine. Nor do they look back to the past in the way that we do as adults, for they are the heirs of the present and the future. The poetry of introspection –

> I remember, I remember
> The house where I was born.
> The little window where the sun

> Came peeping in at morn;
> He never came a wink too soon,
> Nor brought too long a day,
> But now I often wish the night
> Had borne my breath away![1]

– when things past take on a nostalgic meaning and fill the present with sad memories have no place in children's minds.

We, who read aloud the poems we have chosen, will notice, not only the subject matter, the mood and the atmosphere, but also the rhythm, metre and word patterns which the poet has used. Does it sound exciting and alive? Do the words, in fact, sing as we say them? For surely

> Bright is the ring of words
> When the right man rings them,

suggesting the delight and expectancy that the poet himself feels, for in poetry language is at its best. How has the poet used words to convey some special idea or feeling and has he done it successfully? Is the poem too smooth, too jerky, too heavy-footed and clumsy so that the sparkle and vitality have gone, and how do the children respond when they have heard the poem more than once? Poetry written specially for children sometimes – though certainly not always – can imply a looking down on the child as a creature who can only understand and appreciate that which is slightly inferior. A poet must write what he believes in, and he must believe in his own maturity: to toss off immature verses in the expectation that they will do for young children, is to create something which is false and unconvincing.

Children bring the 'innocent eye and the inner ear' to their listening but because of their limited experience they do not know what is there for the taking. We, as adults, must do the providing, the reading aloud, the gift of books or the remembering of a line or verse at the right moment.

As James Reeves suggests in his essay 'Writing poetry for children'[2]:

> The ideal poem for a child is one which at once delights him by

---

[1] Thomas Hood.
[2] From *Young Writers, Young Readers.*

its originality and makes him feel almost as if he might have written it himself. It should enter his consciousness almost unawares and be immediately accepted so that it comes to be something which, like the nursery rhymes of his infancy, he cannot remember ever having not known.

6
Story-telling

Once ... once upon a time.
Over and over again,
Martha would tell her stories
In the hazel glen.
    Walter de la Mare

Down the ages stories have been told and listened to with the greatest of delight. At first man probably drew his tales, showing by his pictures on rocks and in caves what he had done, or what he hoped to do, and by imagining something he wanted to happen, make it come true.

His pictures would tell of his hopes and triumphs, fears and joys. Slowly language must have developed and probably certain individuals in the family or tribe would stand out because of their ability to use words in an exciting and dramatic way.

Tales would gradually grow up around people's early adventures, hunting trips, battles, victories, and a story-teller would be needed to keep these exploits alive so that all could hear them and share vicariously in what had happened. Homer, for example, carried the story of the Trojan Wars all over Greece. During the Middle Ages throughout Europe in the long dark evenings the minstrels and troubadours must have been welcomed with eagerness and relief with their repertoire of songs and stories. In medieval society the idea of childhood as we know it simply did not exist and children, as soon as they could manage without the perpetual care of their mothers, joined adult society: there were no stories specially for them. No doubt, however, they listened to everything they heard.

Today there are plenty of stories written for children, and we know how much they enjoy listening. Yet telling and reading stories to children is something which is sometimes neglected. Parents forget, or are too busy, and yet for the first seven years of a child's life many children do not read sufficiently fluently to read to themselves.

Sometimes at school, at both the nursery and infant school stage, stories get crowded out, for there are so many other things to fit in. It is a great pity if a teacher with a class of children in a nursery school or day nursery does not plan a story time during the day when the children who are ready and eager to listen can come together in a group. Perhaps, because the teacher has not wanted to impose her ideas on young children and interrupt their spontaneous play, she has sometimes tended to say that if her group wants a story, then surely they will come and ask for it. Young children, in fact, often do not know what it is like to sit and listen to a story if the teacher has never shown them how pleasant and stimulating it can be, particularly if they have had no story experiences at home.

It is a mistaken idea of the teacher's, or parent's, role that she should never suggest anything to the children, or make any demands, waiting passively for it all to come from them. In a group of mixed ages it is quite a simple matter to gather those children who are ready and eager for a story – generally the $3\frac{1}{2}$s to 5s – and allow the younger children to play somewhere else in the garden or the passage with one of the young helpers or assistants.

In the infant school, if there are any children in the class who really do not want to listen they too can sit somewhere at the back of the room and play quietly with something else.

One very soon discovers in the nursery those children who are not yet ready for group experiences of this kind and this will not always depend on chronological age. There may be children of three and under who are ready to listen, while some four-year-olds may be too immature to be able to sit quietly for the required time.

If the teacher selects her stories wisely and tells them well, it will not take very long for the children to become settled in a group, listening with real enjoyment, knowing what is expected of them, how they like to sit and what the procedure is. Gradually, as the younger children mature they will want to join the story group too, and by this time certain traditions of behaviour and quiet listening will have developed. It is true that during the nursery day there will probably be brief periods when perhaps one or two children will come and demand a story or bring a favourite book to share with a member of staff, or the teacher herself may go and sit in the book corner, gathering a few children round her to look at something special. This, of course, is an extremely valuable thing for the children concerned, but it is not a sustained period of listening. The busy adult may be called away at any moment to cope with an unexpected situation and therefore it should not take the place of a real story time.

Sometimes, at the end of a long day in a day nursery, young children who are tired may need the warm and quiet intimacy of being read to in an easy and relaxed way when their minds are half on the expected appearance of someone from home and only half on the story.

The story period should be planned to fit into the pattern of the daily programme. If it is left to chance it will probably get left out altogether and then the children will have missed a worthwhile experience. Teachers, too, do not bother to prepare a story which they feel they are unlikely to tell.

Children are not in any way averse to a daily routine which is carefully planned and the time chosen for the story should be one that fits pleasantly and easily into their playtime, music time, meals and rest. Nor do we force reluctant children to come and listen to a story, though if they do come, they are expected to stay and not walk out in the middle. This very rarely happens: children enjoy listening so much that they are the first to complain if they do not get their story, or it is too quickly over. To be comfortable and at peace is as important to listening children as it is to listening adults. We all know how irritating the late-comer to the theatre or concert can be. How maddening, too, to have a good radio or television programme spoilt by the constant comings and goings of the family. It is even more difficult for young children to withstand a flow of interruptions. Their concentration and attention is more easily upset than ours and it takes time and patience to get it back.

Some nursery teachers do sometimes seem to regard a story as something merely to fill up an awkward moment of the day. They tell it, when children are going out to wash for lunch. This means that some children hear the beginning, some the middle and others the end of the story. Doors are opened and closed, there is a scramble for chairs, requests from the staff for the children who have not washed to 'Come at once', and enquiries from the children themselves as to what has happened in the story while they have been away. All this creates confusion and this is certainly not the time for a story. If one has a group at such a moment with nothing special to do, it is quite feasible to look at and talk about individual pictures in a picture book, to sing nursery rhymes or indulge in finger plays. This can be quite amusing and relaxing and children's comings and goings then do not matter.

I do not, of course, mean to imply by this demand for peace and quiet that one cannot tell the children a story except under ideal conditions. One can imagine a group of small children sitting disconsolately waiting for a bus which never comes, or parents who seem indefinitely delayed, even if there is a certain amount of noise and bustle, enjoying the story that the adult is able to produce at a moment's notice. When we have acquired the peace and quiet needed, we should also have forestalled the children's own personal requests by seeing, for example, that everyone is comfortable, that no one needs a hurried visit to the lavatory or a handkerchief extracted from some awkward back pocket, and that if we are going to show pictures while we tell the story, everyone will be able to see them.

In some ways it is more difficult to tell stories to very young children, particularly the under fives than it is to tell them to older children. It is true that the story for the young child is shorter, less complicated, and therefore easier to remember, but whereas the actual drama of the story will often hold the attention of older children, even if it is indifferently told, this does not apply to the under fives. They are very dependent on the personality of the story-teller and her ability to get her story across to them. Their attention wanders easily and they can only sit and listen if their interest is genuinely held.

Through the medium of the story, the story-teller must make them feel happy and at ease, for young children are quick to show their feelings if they are frightened or insecure. They are not prepared to wait a little to see if the story grows more interesting. The story-teller's power of persuasion, her skill in presentation and her own warm friendliness and sympathy must be used to the full from the very beginning. This is one reason why it is so difficult for a complete stranger to come in and tell a story to children in a nursery. She has no real relationship with them and, until she is known and accepted, they regard her with curiosity but not with secure affection and they tend to question her on such things as, 'Where has she come from?' – 'Has she a mummy?' and 'Is she wearing her best shoes?' These speculations naturally interfere with listening. The teacher or nursery assistant, or whoever else is a real part of the establishment, who knows the children individually and has a real link with their homes, is the best person to tell them a story.

A story will be more effective if the listening group is small. Young children particularly should ideally be in a group of about ten to twelve, though of course one would not turn children away. Even with older children it is pleasant to have not more than thirty. In infant and junior schools, of course, the teacher generally has to have the whole class. In the nursery some of the younger children will not be ready to listen but if the group of those who enjoy a story exceeds fifteen then obviously the large number must be accepted, though it is sometimes possible to divide the children into two groups and have two people telling a story while if another room is needed the staff room or medical room can often be used.

There is now a certain number of infant schools where children are grouped vertically, that is, boys and girls of five, six and seven are together in the same class (this is often called "family group-ing") rather than being grouped horizontally according to age. This is often the pattern in the small rural school and is taken for granted, but is something a little new in the ordinary infant school.

Some teachers of family grouped classes are a little anxious lest during story time, if they choose a tale the six- and seven-year-olds will enjoy, the fives may find it too long and complex, whereas, if they try to cater for the fives only the sixes and sevens will be bored. It is, however, quite feasible, and in fact is often done, for teachers to co-operate at story-time, one teacher perhaps taking all the older children in her room, the other teacher taking the younger ones in hers. This means that the whole age range can be satisfied with the right kind of story. There are, of course, certain stories that have a universal appeal and can be enjoyed by the whole group, so, if for some reason a changeover cannot always be arranged, a story of this kind can be chosen.

It would be a great pity, however, if the six- and seven-year-olds never heard the sort of stories they need and enjoy and which stretch and stimulate them imaginatively and intellectually because of the simpler needs of the younger children.

A book corner where children can sit quietly and look at picture and story books is very important in a nursery school, day nursery or infant school. The books should be so arranged in each room, either on a book stand or in a wall-pocket if space is very limited, so that children can see the covers of the books and know what they are choosing. It should be a comfortable place with a table or two to sit at as some picture books are too large and heavy to hold easily in the hands and need to be spread out. The choice should be wide and varied, probably actual information books may be kept near the materials with which they are linked (although this is not always so) – nature books near the nature table, number books, in the infant school, near the number corner. On the whole, therefore, the book corner will probably contain mostly picture books, and in the infant school simple reading books too. Children enjoy sitting and looking at picture books, either alone, or with others with whom they can talk and share experiences. Some infant schools have a library of books set out in the corridors or in an extra room if one is available; sometimes these are reference books shared by the whole school. This gives the children an even wider choice and can be very helpful. On the other hand young children do need books in their own classroom as well, near the security and comfort of their own teacher.

In the book corner children can begin to learn how to take care of books. They can be encouraged to have clean hands and to treat their books carefully; any that are tatty or torn should be removed and mended before the children have them again. Boys and girls in their own homes should have a place to keep their books too, and gradually many of them will build up a library of their own.

It is a mistake to put simple *reading* books into the book corner in the nursery school or day nursery. The children will have these books when they go on to the infant school; they are not ready for books whose main object is the acquiring of the actual skill of learning to read, and to have them too soon takes the gilt off the gingerbread. Books are comforting things and in the book corner children can find release and relaxation and sometimes an escape from the busy activity of the other children.

Telling stories to a group of small children and telling a story to an individual child in a family or substitute family are different propositions.

The child on his own is generally very close to the adult – sometimes sitting on her lap, so that together they can share the pictures and story in a very intimate way. It can be a slow unhurried business for even the smallest illustration can be minutely examined, brooded over and its tiniest detail discovered, for the tempo in the looking and listening is that of the individual child himself. Questions can be asked by the child and answered, and explanations given. The child's own background and experience are often very familiar to the adult, particularly in the ordinary family, so that the picture book chosen is one that will be understood and enjoyed. New words can easily be interpreted and something strange and interesting in a picture can be enlarged upon and its relation to some known experience explained; thus the whole thing can become very meaningful to the child. As the story unfolds he has the adult's individual attention and everything is focused in and around him. As a rule, interruptions only concern himself and the adult can wait in patience until he is ready. As he becomes more accustomed to hearing stories he will be able to enjoy longer and more complicated ones, for he will have built up within himself the ability to listen until an end is reached.

In the family there is often a variety of times during the day when it can be story-time and tales can be long or short according to the child's own pleasure. Stories to fit going to bed and being bathed and other day to day happenings are always enjoyed by children, and they often delight in a story that is woven around them and their doings. Some of these stories will obviously have to be made up by the adult if they are to be concerned with the child himself.

It would be a great pity if television or radio programmes squeezed out family reading and story-telling. A book read aloud, perhaps on a wet or winter evening, is a lovely experience. It may be one that the under seven cannot really understand though it is possible for everyone to take it in turn to choose. Perhaps, however, the very young are on the fringe of the group playing quietly but listening too, and accepting that which they are ready for and able to take. They are still individually free to come and go, and yet are a part of the listening family. They often get the feel and flavour of a book which they are too young to understand fully. Later on, when they are ready, they rediscover it as a familiar friend, full of half-remembered things and bound up with warm, happy memories.

The child who for some reason is away from home, perhaps because his parents are unable or unwilling to keep him, may find great comfort in the intimacy of a story told, perhaps just for him. He may be able to make his first real relationship with an adult who is telling the tale. He can be greedy and demanding showing his need for attention and his need to be the only one and have all the love. Who knows what memories the story or rhyme may awaken in his mind, what the pictures in the book signify! The aggressive child may feel a little more at peace – the withdrawn child make some outward sign indicating his longing for affection and notice. At bedtime, in bed, or in front of the fire in the playroom, one or perhaps two children can enjoy an intimate and relaxed time with an adult, away from the noise and bustle of the rest of the group. Such times are extremely informal, but just because there can be this close contact between a child, or two children and an adult, they can be very comforting.

It is just as important to have a story evening with children in a children's home as it is in the ordinary family; with older children a continued tale can be read and the smaller ones can often have their turn first when something easy is provided. It is surprising how often even the bigger boys and girls enjoy listening to one of the simple stories they used to know when they were small, though they probably wouldn't admit to their enjoyment of it.

If a child is ill in bed, to find time to share a picture book or read to him, helps one to get to know him better. Barriers tend to come down, sometimes with even the most awkward of children, and one gets a glimpse of what lies behind the façade of the hostile, shy, selfish and unlovable boy or girl. They may ask questions or offer information which may give us a key to their problems. To trust a child with a precious book may mean, too, the beginning of a new and happier relationship.

The experience of telling or reading stories to children whether as individuals or in groups is something that we, as adults, can enjoy as much as the listening children, for we shall not only be reminded of old childhood favourites – we shall find ourselves discovering all kinds of new and exciting material unwritten when we were young.

What sort of stories are suitable to tell or read to groups of nursery and infant school children? Various kinds of story and the subject matter involved have already been discussed. We know that children want drama and a simple straightforward plot, that the story will have a beginning, a middle and an end, work up to its climax and have an emotionally satisfying finish.

We may choose to read our story from a book sometimes showing the pictures as we do so. We may, on the other hand, just tell the story without the aid of pictures at all. In a group of young children, particularly if they are unaccustomed to hearing stories, to look at pictures and listen at the same time can be difficult and distracting. Also, unless the illustrations are fairly large and clear, children cannot always see them distinctly and are unable to make out the details which they find so fascinating. Our story should obviously be one that has literary qualities. Adults often make up stories to tell to young children, and probably many of us have wonderful memories of those our parents or relatives told us, perhaps about themselves when they were young, or tales made up out of their own heads. This is often ideal in the family situation and many published children's books were first told and retold to the writer's own children. It is something to be careful about, however, with a group of children. Indifferent and second-rate material is sometimes handed out to young children, just because the adult cannot be bothered to find a real story from a book. Whatever story we do tell, it should be one that we ourselves like and enjoy, otherwise we shall tell it without any real conviction. Children often want a story repeated and to have to do this with a story we dislike is very wearisome.

Language is a means of communication; through its use children can make friends, explain their wants, settle their differences, ask questions, offer help and comfort to each other. It gives them a feeling of confidence to use language easily and well. We all know how devastating it can be when we find ourselves surrounded by people who do not understand a word we say. It is often necessary to help children to talk freely and spontaneously to each other and to adults when they first come to nursery or infant school, and we must talk to them freely and naturally ourselves.

Nowadays children are not taught the actual mechanics of reading until they can express themselves in words as the result of direct experiences. To read without meaning, like a parrot, is quite valueless to both children and adults; the printed word only has significance if we understand it. Many of us could, perhaps, read a page of print in a foreign language by imagining the sounds of the symbols but of what use would it be to us if we did not know what it meant? It could be the beginning of a story, a cooking recipe or a manual on first aid and we should be none the wiser. Children gain language experiences in their free, self-chosen play as well as when they listen to stories and poetry or talk about the picture books they are looking at.

A story, of course, should not be altered to suit a particular group of children. If it is felt to be too difficult, too sad, to contain incidents that the children will not understand or which the adult feels embarrassed about telling, then it should be left untold until the children are older. Not only is it unfair to the creator of the story to alter it but later on, if children hear the correct version, they feel both confused and cheated. Nor should we ever give children either young or old, 'potted' and 'watered down' classics – *Alice in Wonderland*, *Oliver Twist* or *Jane Eyre* produced as strip cartoons. Here something of real worth is being given to children in such a form that it is utterly ruined and to imagine that boys and girls are hearing the classics when the qualities that make them, their language and style, characterization and freshness are lost, is quite absurd and an insult to the author, the story and the child.

Another mistake that adults are inclined to make is in the telling of Bible Stories to young children. Many grown-ups imagine there is a kind of magic about such stories that will enable children not only to get so-called religious instruction from them but also to receive some form of moral training and to understand them when in fact they deal with ideas, feelings and experiences quite beyond their comprehension.

60

A Bible story or Bible picture book should be judged in exactly the same way as any other story or picture book we present to young children, solely on its merits and the suitability of its subject matter as a story and the quality of its illustrations as a picture book, remembering that it will have no moral or religious significance to a young child except in so far as he is able to accept and enjoy the values – kindness, security, love, generosity, fun, etc. – with which the tale is concerned. To talk about God before a child has any experience to which this word corresponds can only disturb and bewilder him. Even up to seven or eight, recent research has tended to show, children appear unable to grasp religious ideas.

As Dr R. S. Lee says in his book, *The Growing Child and Religion*:

> The aim of religious education then, is not to constrain the child to become religious, but to ensure that as he comes to maturity of development he will find in religion the fullest expression of his inward self. We must not assume without question that the best way to achieve this is to train the child from the beginning in the forms of religion – prayers, Bible stories, children's services and so on. The child may find great interest in all these, but his interest will be of a social, intellectual and aesthetic character, not religious.

So, if we tell Bible stories to children they will not have any real religious significance and we tell them simply as exciting and dramatic tales. Stories such as Noah's Ark (omitting the idea of a revengeful and punishing God) and Moses in the bulrushes, can be enjoyed by many young children. The Christmas story is probably regarded by most modern boys and girls as a magic tale associated with presents, Christmas trees, Santa Claus, decorations, and lots to eat, yet this need not spoil its charm and delight.

Young children are also very easily confused by the supernatural element in many Bible stories. On the one hand they are often told that these stories are true, and on the other they hear tales which to them seem full of the magic of fantasy and cannot exist in reality. Older children and adults are generally able to recognize the symbolism in many of the Old and New Testament stories but young children find this very difficult to interpret either in terms of the real or the make believe. Added to this, religion is a subject so emotionally charged to many people that they cannot look at it rationally.

Adults who are honestly religious, and wish to give their children a religious upbringing, need to be particularly careful in this respect for in their anxiety to accomplish this task they are sometimes tempted to tell and read Bible stories or underline a moral which only bewilders and confuses their children. In any case boys and girls incorporate true goodness within themselves by example rather than by precept. Human beings can only discover whatever faith or philosophy of life they need and try to live by through personal experience and growth and this is the task of a lifetime.

Yet, the Bible, like Shakespeare, is part of our cultural and literary heritage and as such we want our children, when they are ready, to know and enjoy its exciting and dramatic stories, understand it as part of the history of humankind, delight in its language and poetry and absorb many of its values.

Many of use feel no longer able to accept the divinity of Christ and Christianity as such as a personal faith. We would not, therefore, interpret Bible stories in a religious way, thinking of them rather in their historical setting with their often symbolic meaning, and if we imagine that we can pass on to children beliefs which we ourselves no longer hold, we are making a very grave mistake. It is also only too easy to put children off the real truths in religion by quite unsuitable teaching, by giving them sentimental picture books, or watered down, pious little moral tales, or by expecting them to take part in religious group experiences for which they are not ready or are unwilling to participate in.

Another kind of story that causes some parents a little worry, though very different in significance from the Bible story, is the legend of Father Christmas. What do we say to the children, for example, when they ask questions about this famous old gentleman? Nowadays boys and girls see so many rather tatty old men with long white beards and red gowns wandering about the big stores at Christmas time. Which of these elderly figures will come down their chimney on Christmas Eve loaded with presents? If a young child asks, in all good faith, if Father Christmas is really true, what are we going to say? Perhaps the best way of dealing with such a question is to throw it back to the child saying, 'Well, what do you think?' and in his reply we shall get some idea of what is troubling him. If he is really bewildered and wants an answer from us, then I think, in all honesty, we must say, 'Well I think, don't you, that Father Christmas is really Daddy and I (or Daddy and Mummy) who buy presents and put them ready for you to find on Christmas morning, but it's rather fun to pretend there is a Father Christmas who has a sledge drawn by reindeer and who comes down the chimney with a sack of toys on his back'.

Children enjoy believing in this sort of magic even when they know it is only 'pretend', and they have a wonderful capacity for slipping in and out of the world of reality and fantasy. One moment they know Father Christmas is only 'pretend', the next they are wondering what sort of letter they are going to write to him and what gifts he will cram in their stockings or pillowcases.

Older children will often talk about Father Christmas with a twinkle in their eye as much as to say, 'I know this is all hooey, but it's fun'. We certainly do not want to spoil young children's sense of expectancy and delight, for we must always tread warily when children's fantasies are concerned.

We need not feel too serious about this, for probably without any particular enlightenment from us, and no anxiety on the part of the child, Father Christmas will, like Lewis Carroll's Boojum, simply vanish away when he is no longer needed.

7

Techniques of Story-telling

I would rather be the children's story-teller than the Queen's favourite or the King's counsellor.

Kate Douglas Wiggin

The actual techniques of story-telling are important and although we all bring our own individuality to our telling of a tale, there are certain basic things we should bear in mind and certain pitfalls we should avoid. First of all a group of children must be able to hear what is being said and, although some people are blessed with a more pleasing voice than others, children are not too critical in this respect.

We must, of course, use our voices expressively, articulating clearly with changes of pitch and speed. The amount of expression a story-teller puts into her voice is a little dependent on the age of the children and the kind of story she is telling. Children do enjoy it very much when, with a slight change of voice, we seem to become the characters in the story we are telling. The gruff voice of father bear when he is demanding, 'Who has been eating my porridge?', or the rather squeaky little voice for baby bear as he protests about his porridge, or the chair Goldilocks has broken, helps to make the story live for children. But expression should not be exaggerated, for just as words can take on a new pleasure when they are heard and their meaning becomes more emotionally charged through the medium of the human voice, so their frightening quality can be felt more vividly also. If one is reading a book and one becomes scared, it can be put down, a radio or television programme can be turned off. Children, however, often cannot get away from the adult who is telling or reading a story to them with such shiver-making and frightening qualities in her voice, they can hardly bear it, for it must be remembered that the story-teller is not an actor. On the other hand, of course, the slightly older child – the six- or seven-year-old –

enjoys feeling a little scared, particularly in a group when all the other children are feeling scared too.

Gesture is something that can help to make or mar a story. If it is overdone, children may sit spellbound, but they are probably wondering what queer things the adult is going to do next and have quite lost the thread of the tale. I remember once seeing a story-teller mount a chair and stand on tiptoe to try to convey to a group of children how high the trees were in the forest she was describing; the children, sitting breathless with astonishment, were obviously waiting for her to fall off.

Sometimes a gesture is so slight it is felt rather than seen, while the merest movement, the lift of an eyebrow, the shake of a head, can tell children quite a lot. How gesture is used will vary very much from person to person; some people use their hands and bodies much more than others to express their feelings.

I remember hearing a young teacher tell 'The Tale of the Turnip' to a group of four- and five-year-olds. Almost everything she said was accompanied by the use of her hands and body. She put on imaginary clothes, took them off, dug in the garden, planted the turnip seed, put the tools away, set the table, etc. It sounds somewhat exaggerated, but in actual fact it was delightful. Everything she did was so much a part of herself, so natural, easy and alive that the children loved it all.

Whether we speak slowly or quickly will depend on what is actually happening in our story. We quicken up the pace when something exciting occurs, when something is moving faster and faster, or there is the feel of hurry and bustle in the air. We speak more slowly when we want to emphasize a particular phrase or convey its imaginative quality to a child. If something sad happens we shall tend to describe it more quietly and slowly and to take conversations at the speed which seems to suit the characters who are speaking. A pause can be most effective if it helps to heighten the suspense. Pauses before a character speaks, or after a particularly imaginative passage are also impressive. A pause will make it clear which character is speaking and it also gives children time to finish thinking about one idea before going on to the next. Certain words and phrases will be made to sound more important and significant than others and we shall want children to feel when the climax has

65

been reached.

Young children love repetition. Sometimes it may be just the repeating of a new word which will help to impress it on their minds. At other times, a dearly loved sentence in which they can join – 'No, no, by the hair of my chinny chin chin' – and they wait with delight for such phrases to occur, join in at the appropriate moment, and then wait for the next.

It may seem unnecessary to suggest that the story-teller should know the tale she is going to tell, but this is not as simple as it sounds. Not only must she remember the incidents in their right order and the tiny details about the characters that bring them to life; she has also to clothe the bare bones of her tale in language that is rich and imaginative.

We shall all learn to remember our stories in our own way, but a half-remembered tale with an important incident omitted, or slight changes that may seem immaterial to us, can spoil the story for the children.

If we have a group of children we should plan our story-telling periods ahead so that we know what we are going to tell. This does not mean that we cannot change our minds, but I have seen so many adults pick up the first book that comes to hand and use it, regardless of its real suitability, just because it happens to be the nearest one within reach. If we plan ahead, keeping notes on the stories told, particularly if there is more than one version, we shall also be able to choose poetry to read or say which will fit in with the atmosphere of the tale. We shall know, too, how often we repeat a story either by our own wish or at the children's request and whether we are forgetting to tell any special story which no child should miss.

If we get individual children who appear to lose interest, fidget and disturb the others, it is sometimes possible to draw them back into the tale without causing a lot of commotion. It can be rather upsetting to everyone if we make a dramatic stop and show our displeasure. Instead, by mentioning the child's name as if this bit of the story was especially his, we can sometimes draw him effectively back into the group. Then we must do our best to hold his attention. If this continues to happen with one or two children, however, and the remainder of the group are at ease, it may mean that these children are not yet ready for this kind of experience and would be happier doing something else.

The skilful adult takes it for granted that children are going to be co-operative, want a story and want to listen quietly. So often one gets from human beings what one expects, and if one thinks children are going to be tiresome and awkward, then they often are. Sometimes a group contains one or two very energetic and lively four- and five-year-old boys who always seem to be busy doing something else at story time and although no one wants to interrupt a very vital bit of play, it is a great pity if such children miss out on stories altogether. These children constitute a challenge to any story-teller, and if one can gently but firmly persuade them into listening once or twice, it does not take very long, if the stories are exciting and well-chosen, for these children to become the most fervent and eager of listeners.

We may not always realize how important human eyes are when telling children stories. The children themselves fasten their eyes on us and we, on our part, look at them – not only to find out how they are responding but because we shall express in our eyes some of the things we are feeling: the sparkle of laughter, the sadness of pity and compassion, the indignation of anger, the excitement of interest and surprise.

It is not wise to ask children questions in a story, though story-tellers do sometimes resort to this if they think they are losing the interest of their group – 'And what do you think the pussy did then?' we say hopefully. Alas, young children rarely give one the correct or hoped-for answer, for their fertile imaginations suggest all sorts of possibilities we had never envisaged. Once children start suggesting undreamed of and impossible answers, those who have no ideas on the subject at all soon become bored. They begin to fidget, tip their chairs, play with each other and instead of getting the attention we had hoped for, whatever atmosphere we had achieved utterly vanishes. We shall probably have to stop altogether, get everyone quiet and make a new beginning.

Sometimes children enjoy a tale that revolves round a puppet or a doll that can be made to behave in a realistic and lively way, and sometimes special objects that are mentioned in the story can be shown to the children. The adult who draws easily and skilfully may

67

perhaps illustrate the tale as it is being told, or a flanelgraph can be used in the same way. One does not need to use these devices all the time but just occasionally children enjoy them.

Of course we must never talk down to children in that somewhat arch and skittish way that at one time was the fashion. Children should be spoken to as equals and we laugh with them, not at them. It is of course wonderful at the end of a well told tale to get that breathless hush when the children show, not by words, but by that satisfied silence, how much they have enjoyed it. Then, whatever trouble we have taken in finding and preparing our story, we shall feel amply rewarded.

A Story Diary

I decided it would be an enjoyable experience to tell some stories to a small group of under fives. I have in the past told a great many stories to children of this age but I have never written about it. I have also always known the children I was telling these stories to, very well.

This particular group of twelve children between the ages of four and five I saw only when I went into the day nursery with my picture books twice a week, and I did not do anything else with them. They were a mixed group of nine girls and three boys, and varied in size, general appearance and ability to listen. As they were attending a day nursery, their hours were long and there were problems of various kinds at home.

Florrie was a thin, fragile-looking child, poorly dressed with enormous blue eyes in a rather frightened little face. She was not very demanding and tended to draw away if one put one's arm round her. She had a straight fringe which made her face look even smaller.

Sheila was a well-dressed and well cared for child with glasses, rather quiet and a little aloof but eager, as a rule, to listen.

Danny was a big rosy-cheeked, black-haired boy, tall for his age, slow of speech but very anxious to talk of his own concerns and with a grim determination to go on until he had finished, regardless of the remarks of the other children.

Tommy, small and plump, found it difficult to keep still and what he enjoyed doing most was to tip his chair until he slid off onto the ground where he caused a commotion amongst everyone's feet.

Pauline was one of those children one tends not to notice; she sank into herself, particularly as she almost always sat herself next to Pippa who was very demanding of notice.

Pippa was a big, dark child – restless and fidgety. She found it difficult to keep her mind and her arms and her legs from wandering all over the place. She played with the children near her so that they forgot to listen and her attention was distracted by the slightest thing.

Hilda was one of those fair, round-faced children – comfortable, plump, eager for notice, rather important; she generally had something to say, confiding and loving.

Janet also was short and plump, but dark-haired and full of giggles and laughter, quick to join in a joke and continue laughing when everyone else had finished. She showed real interest in the story and remembered what she had heard.

Jane was a tall, attractive child with dark blue eyes; she was rather quiet but every now and then she would suddenly slip her hand in mine and smile.

Dickie was a small, thin boy with a thatch of dark hair; he did not always appear very interested in the story and sometimes stayed away.

Mollie, a very blonde little creature, always brought a doll with her to which she held on tightly whenever any of the other children offered to hold it for her. She and Ella, a rather skinny, eager-faced child, always sat together and sometimes held hands. They often decided to take off their cardigans with a great deal of fuss, either just as I was about to begin the story or when I was well and truly started. This was my group!

MONDAY

The group as a whole was friendly, eager and welcoming, a little clinging and demanding of attention in some form or other. They interrupted frequently, particularly when they remembered something they wanted to say; they would embark on it immediately, whatever point the story had reached. One interruption tended to distract everyone's attention. Pippa and Danny, in particular, only half listened to what was being said.

It is always a little difficult with a group of children that one sees only occasionally, particularly when one does not participate in their other activities, for young children really need a much closer, more frequent and continuous relationship. One tended to be an excitement and novelty for much too long, instead of becoming a part of their daily lives.

We started off with finger plays which they did not know.

> Two little dickie birds
> Sat upon a wall,
> One named Peter
> And one named Paul.
> Fly away Peter,
> Fly away Paul.
> Come back Peter,
> Come back Paul.

followed by,

> These are mother's knives and forks,
> And this is mother's table,
> This is mother's looking glass
> And here's the baby's cradle.

This held and absorbed them; they tried hard to get it right and kept correcting each other. 'Danny has it wrong.' 'I can't get my hands up high.'

I started off with Marjorie Flack's *Angus Lost*, but had not realized until I began that they found it difficult to see the pictures, the room was an awkward shape and the chairs badly arranged. They kept asking 'What's that?' at almost every picture and this made the story disjointed and some of them lost the thread. But it is a very simple story and they got back to the point again in the end.

Every picture seemed to remind them of some event in their own lives about which they wanted to talk. I think the story was enjoyed for its novelty rather than for anything else.

TUESDAY

I was met with cries of welcome and everyone hurried into the special room – Danny and Tommy both insisting on wearing their caps. Hilda was full of the coming of her mother, and she kept saying 'Mother's coming in the afternoon'; at this, Danny started chanting, 'afternoon, noon, noon', and soon everyone was saying, 'noon, noon, noon, noon', Janet being convulsed with laughter.

We did our finger plays and then I said I was going to tell them a story about a little boy called Danny who wanted to find a birthday present for his mother. (Another of Marjorie Flack's stories.)

Danny was very forthcoming about himself, his age, his birthday; he counted up on his fingers to show me he was four. I started off on 'Ask Mr Bear', but this time I had no pictures to distract the children and I could watch their faces. The end of the story where Danny gives his mother a 'bear hug' fell a little flat and I felt the children did not know what I meant, although I had woven the explanation of a 'bear hug' into the story and had demonstrated it by hugging Hilda.

They enjoyed the repetition and kept saying, 'My mummy has an egg', 'My mummy has a feather pillow' etc., whenever Danny is offered these things as presents by the different animals he meets. I was not at all sure how much it had been enjoyed.

MONDAY

We started off with a new finger play.

> Ten little squirrels sitting on a tree,
> These two said, 'What can we see?'
> These two said 'A man with a gun'.
> These two said 'Let's run, let's run'.
> These two said 'Let's hide in the shade',
> These two said, 'We're not afraid'.
> And the gun went 'Bang' and away they all ran.

This, and the other ones they had learned kept everyone busy. I then told them 'The Three Bears', a story they all knew, thinking perhaps they would join in where the repetition comes, but there was a deadly silence.

Then I reminded them of Danny's birthday present to his mother and asked what it was. Janet immediately said, 'A bear hug', and flung her arms round my neck; several of the others joined in, so I think they had probably enjoyed it.

TUESDAY

We started off with the familiar finger plays again and then I told them 'The Three Little Pigs' which they had heard before, but this time everyone joined in when the repetition came. There were moments in the story when I felt that I had got them but Danny and Tommy were very restless. Tommy, particularly, would stretch out his arms wide to show the size of the little pig's house, hitting the children on either side of him; this made him laugh and he got very excited and tipped his chair forward so that he fell on the floor. My nice atmosphere went as Tommy grovelled among everyone's feet. Still, the story had its brief moments.

MONDAY

Today I taught them a new face game: 'Knock at the door' (knock on your forehead), 'Pull the bell' (pull your ears), 'Peep through the key hole' (screw up your eyes), 'Lift the latch' (pull up your nose), 'Walk in' (open your mouth, letting your finger walk in). They adored it and kept saying, 'Do it again, Do it again', until we had done it a dozen times or more. I chose an unsuccessful story in that there was not enough drama in it to hold them. It was an American one of a little boy called Wakey who never wanted to go to bed. The animals all showed him how they slept. Finally Wakey decided that his way of going to bed was best for him. Mollie and Ella took off their cardigans and the moment they had taken them off they proceeded to put them on again. Dickie crawled round the backs of the chairs and silently removed some beads Hilda was wearing. She wept in protest and I felt my story was a failure. We returned to our face games and order was restored.

TUESDAY

We started with the face game which aroused passionate interest and we repeated it again and again.

Then I told them a 'Mr Buffin' story. Mr Buffin is a kindly grey-haired old gentleman who has sundry adventures with his horse, cat, garden, etc. I like him, because I do not know of any other series of tales that brings in a kindly old gentleman. 'He's just like my grandad', said Pamela and this is a comment children often make.

The story of 'Ink the Cat' who got on the breakfast table and put his head in the milk jug because Mr Buffin overslept and did not come down in time to give Ink his breakfast called forth 'Ohs' and

'Ahs' of disapproval, especially when Ink knocks things off the table.

When I said that Mr Buffin was getting himself an alarm clock to wake him in the morning everyone said they had an alarm clock too, and there was the pinging of many bells. These children are always very anxious to tell me, sometimes in the very middle of the story, things about home. Perhaps because they are away from home for rather a long time, talking about things connected with mother makes them feel happy and secure.

MONDAY

Today I really felt for the first time that the children welcomed me with love and enjoyment.

I told them the story of 'Timid Timothy' which is the tale of a kitten who is afraid of everything. His mother tells him to arch his back, fluff up his fur and wave his tail and go psss whenever he is frightened. He has all sorts of adventures and is always having to say psss, and this the children found really exciting, and at the right moment they, too, all said psss – it was a real success.

TUESDAY

Today, after our usual finger plays and face games, I told the children the story of *Peter Rabbit*. I do not know whether they had heard it before; I believe just one or two of them had, but it made no difference to their rapt enjoyment. They hung on my words with their eyes glued to mine and a breathless interest on their faces.

At the end, there was that momentary hush and then an almost audible sigh of satisfaction as of an experience enjoyed and completed. There was a feeling of warmth and intimacy between us. No one noticed when the door was quietly opened and then closed again.

'Tell us another', said Janet, and I knew that all was well.

8

Nursery Rhymes

To attempt to justify nursery rhymes would be as silly as an attempt to justify Dutch dolls, cowslips, solemn infant faces, mermaids or moonshine. Like speedwell, daisy, chickweed, and shepherd's weather glass and heartsease, they are the exquisite wild weeds of the inexhaustible garden of poetry.

Walter de la Mare

Nursery rhymes have already been mentioned briefly in the chapter on poetry particularly in relation to sound, rhythm and action – qualities which always appeal to young children. Perhaps, however, a little more should be said about them. Nursery rhymes emerge from a past world, lacking in prudery and with an acceptance of tolerance, pain, violence and death as a part of life for us all, young and old. They are children's heritage for they help them to discover all sorts of things about themselves, their own lives and those of others. Young children accept and understand what they are needing at the moment of time when they hear or read the nursery rhyme.

The language of nursery rhymes is rich and exuberant with the frequent use of synonyms (words denoting the same thing). So children can enjoy a 'misty, moisty morning' or a 'cold and frosty' one and meet old men whose clothes are both tattered and torn. They learn face and body games. They meet characters who prance, amble, wander, spin, go milking, make jam tarts and eat peas pudding and curds and whey. They are introduced to cock horses and unicorns and real horses too when they hear that you

> Shoe the little horse,
> Shoe the little mare,
> But let the little colt go bare, bare, bare.

In fact, kindness to animals is emphasized in a world in which it was probably singularly absent. Children learn to love little pussy and not to pull her tail or drive her away. Who could spurn a dejected kitten who comes to your door in need?

> Whose that ringing at my door bell?
> A little pussy cat who isn't very well!
> Rub her little nose with a bit of mutton fat
> That's what you do to a little pussy cat.

Whether this treatment acts as a cure for a sick kitten I have no idea but at least it shows interest and concern.

Topsyturvy rhymes help children to spot the differences between sense and nonsense.

> The man in the moon
> Came down too soon
> And asked his way to Norwich.
> He went by the south
> And burnt his mouth
> While supping cold plum porridge.

What new worlds, too, are spread before children when making their first journey abroad in fantasy:

> How many miles to Babylon?
> Three score and ten,
> Can I get there by candle light?
> Yes, and back again.

Or, suddenly and unexpectedly, discovering a silver nutmeg and a golden pear, a gift from the fairies.

Love and marriage have their romantic side and the very young start early in life, in their own light-hearted fashion, to have their sweethearts. What could be pleasanter than to 'sit on a cushion and sew a fine seam and feed upon strawberries, sugar and cream'? Not perhaps a very reliable picture of married life, but a truly desirable one.

The idea of death is something young children cannot understand. If a loved person dies, it appears to them as a rejection of themselves: 'Mother or father wouldn't have deserted me if they had really loved me. Why have they done this and what have I done to deserve it?' Yet, as a concept, death is a reality and something we all have to try and come to terms with, sooner or later, hard though it is. To hear of it casually, however, without the trauma attached to a loved person, introduces children to the idea in a casual, yet realistic way, particularly if it is once removed, as it were, and if it applies to birds or animals. When the old grey goose dies it is sad to think of her little goslings, 'Who have to scratch for their own bread', but in any case she was destined to become a feather bed. When cock robin is killed the sorrows of the bird population and all the business associated with his burial add a sense of drama to the whole proceedings. Gradually the word becomes a part of children's vocabulary and they begin to understand a tiny fraction of what it all involves.

To children's great delight there are a lot of very badly behaved boys and girls in the nursery rhymes and they contain, too, a measure of violence and law breaking. This links children with their own aggressive and destructive fantasies. Actually, no child is likely to throw a silly old man downstairs by his left leg because he does not say his prayers, run off with a pig, or sit among the cinders. To share, through identification, in these exciting misdeeds is very comforting. Naturally the wrong-doers are beaten and punished for their misdeeds and this is very desirable; justice is seen to be done.

To sleep when you should be working, like Little Boy Blue, to go to bed with your trousers on and one shoe off, to try and catch a whale in a bucket, well, 'it's foolish but it's fun'.

We are not all mathematical and later on at school many children find dealing with figures somewhat daunting; but at least the beginnings of number has its delights and compensations:

> One, two, buckle my shoe,
> Three, four, knock at the door,
> Five, six, pick up sticks,
> Seven, eight, lay them straight,
> Nine, ten, a good fat hen,
> Eleven, twelve, dig and delve.

It is a useful accomplishment also to be ready to count your cherries when you eat them.

> One two three four,
> Mary at the cottage door.
> Five six seven eight,
> Eating cherries off the plate.

There are counting rhymes in plenty which introduce children to real life situations and the rhymes themselves help children to remember the way the numbers run. Here is mathematics without tears.

Some nursery rhymes involve sharing games and everyone can go round the mulberry bush or fall down at the appropriate moment when playing ring-a-ring-o'-roses. So, here are the beginnings of play which involve older children, but at the same time there is no forcing of social relationships for which young children are not yet ready. The world of everyday things means much to a growing child and there is a sense of wonder in all the simple delights which adults no longer find very interesting.

To hear the clock strike one and think of a mouse; to put the kettle on for tea with Polly; to laugh with the dish that ran away with the spoon; to share Little Bo-Peep's anxiety; or to find a ladybird in the garden who should be hurrying home to her children for the house is on fire – is really enthralling. In nursery rhymes children discover a world in miniature in which they can share, explore, and enjoy to their hearts' content. As parents and teachers we must ensure that they have easy access to this enchanting paradise.

9

Bias in Children's Books

Read not to contradict and confute, nor to believe and take for granted, nor to find talk and discourse, but to weigh and consider.
Francis Bacon

Bias, how does the Oxford Dictionary define this particular word? It is described as: to influence (usually unfairly) or an inclination, a predisposition or a prejudice towards a subject or object.

Adults are often biased, particularly in relation to the wishes and needs of children, feeling that they are older and wiser. Adults know best how children should be fed, clothed, taught, how they should behave, what they should learn and what books and stories they should read and enjoy.

There is no general agreement among adults – opinions differ widely, but we all tend to think that those who differ from us are obviously biased in their opinions – in relation to which picture and story books should be provided for young children. Personal prejudices become apparent when discussing how children's books are illustrated; their content; how they are presented and used. Children tend to be at the mercy of those who spend the money, the publishers who produce the books, the latest fashion that has somehow caught on, the power of advertising and the costs of production.

Children often like picture and story books which many so-called knowledgeable adults deplore. The Topsy and Tim books, for example, are seized on eagerly by small children with delighted pleasure. They enjoy the rather flat, repetitive pictures which present no problems and where the same family takes part in ordinary, everyday experiences, somewhat boring, unimaginative and uninspired, to many adults.

There is no need here to say anything more about some people's bias against Little Black Sambo, as I have already referred to this in a previous chapter. It is enough to repeat what a well-loved story this is, enhancing children's admiration of coloured children as shown by the charm and cleverness of this delightful little boy.

However, perhaps the author who causes most controversy and concern (some librarians will not have her books on their shelves) is Enid Blyton. Why do so many children name her as their favourite author and avidly read everything she has written? Her stories are often snobbish in outlook and the children in them who are poor or who come from other countries are generally those who are unpleasant, selfish and disagreeable. Yet Enid Blyton provides children with an escape into a dream world – a world we all long for and need; a world where children can identify themselves with clever and resourceful characters who have wonderful adventures and who always appear as the heroes and heroines of the tales, outwitting the slow, rather stupid and often self-opinionated adults. Actually, I doubt very much whether Helen Bannerman or Enid Blyton really influence children's opinions in regard to colour, race or background.

We all have certain ideas that exertion is associated with virtue; anything which is easy is suspect. Stories, particularly those that deal with children's fantasies, are feared because of their wishful nature. Yet in such stories we can all satisfy impulses and desires which in actual daily life are often unacceptable and must be denied. Both adults and children find in the stories they read and the pictures they look at what they are looking for in life at that particular moment in time. The boys and girls who enjoy Helen Bannerman and Enid Blyton are not concerned with the problems of race, colour or privilege, but with their own longings and dreams, to be clever, grown up, and to do all those things that life will probably continue to deny them.

It is rather the society in which a child grows up, the opinions and attitudes of parents which are continually presented to him or her which will affect the child's thinking and behaviour. In any case children are provided, if not at home at least at school, with a great variety of picture and story books to help them sort out their own feelings and needs and so to come to terms with some of the conflicts and stresses life will present to them.

Many of us may have elusive memories of our own childhood, but are perhaps unaware how these early experiences affect the way we feel and react today. We may peer into the pit of our memory but it is sometimes too deep for us to discover what lies below. Yet the characters that walk through the pages of the stories we read and the pictures we look at are different aspects of ourselves. To stir the pool of our memory and rediscover our childhood's pleasures and sorrows, anxieties and needs, aggressions and fears can be an enlightenment for all of us, even if in the process we unearth a sleeping 'dragon' we did not really wish to disturb and whose existence we had almost forgotten. Our early memories can threaten us, appearing in a new but half-recognizable form when we look at today's picture books and stories. Perhaps the 'dragon' has only been dozing and turned in its sleep, but it has been enough to haunt and disturb us.

I know, for example, that I am prejudiced when I look at Maurice Sendak's *Where the Wild Things Are* (Puffin) and find it uncomfortably disturbing because of its personal reminders; for as a young child I had a recurring nightmare: in the flickering half-light in my bedroom a strange creature with large bare feet would pad towards me. I could see the shadows of long arms and fingers reflected on the walls. I could hear the eerie sound of huge naked feet slowly padding beside my bed with a face half-hidden and I would scream with terror. I know that in the story in *Where the Wild Things Are* Max, the small boy, was in control of the wild things he had dreamed in a way I could never command the monster who paced my room. But the pictures of those mysterious Wild Things with animal heads and human feet still trigger off some of my early feelings of terror. Other picture books by Maurice Sendak I find delightful and exhilarating. I have shared with children real enjoyment and pleasure with *In the Night Kitchen* (Puffin).

If we can recognize in ourselves some of our reasons and reactions to certain picture books and stories we can at least bring a more rational judgment to bear on our looking at and reading of material written for children. Naturally, the reverse can often happen as our memories are not always frightening and unpleasant and we may be reminded instead of the delights of our childhood and of the picture books and stories we enjoyed so much. We may need to be careful here, not necessarily to expect children to like the books we loved when we were young. Many of them may be somewhat dated in style, language and content. On the other hand, there are, what we think of as the 'children's classics', those books which possess that almost indefinable quality of freshness generally irresistible to the boys and girls of today.

It is interesting to observe that although today's child readers will probably be tomorrow's adult readers and buyers of books, and so need to be 'hooked on books' early in life, little attempt seems to be made in the great majority of bookshops or large stores (except those catering mainly for children) to display their wares in ways which will attract boys and girls. Quite often the children's books are squeezed into a small corner. Many of them are awkward to get at, either too high or so low one has to grovel on the floor – what one might call 'a mouse's eye view'. When only the backs of books are visible children often do not know what a title signifies. It might therefore be more helpful if paper and hardback books were arranged according to subject i.e. school, historical, magic, animal, science fiction etc.

As for poetry books, they are often hidden away in some obscure corner which is almost impossible to find and generally out of reach. There is rarely a table and chairs where children can sit and look at books for themselves at their leisure. There is rarely an assistant at hand to help or advise. In a large London store – which shall be nameless – it took me quite a time to find someone who could help me locate a well-known book for children. When I eventually discovered the individual who was in charge of the children's books, I got no help whatsoever and so came out, minus the book.

We tend to think of children as miniature adults old enough to look for what they want themselves – and, of course, they are not. They have their own special needs and wishes and they often react neither as we do nor as we expect. Naturally adults can be extremely wise and helpful when, by careful questioning, they discover the kind of book a child is looking for and wants.

We would all agree that picture books and stories for young children should not contain scenes or descriptions which would terrify or pervert; or provide books of information that are grossly inaccurate. In general, Western society feels that whatever is wished for in adult literature should be accepted but the children's books should be censored for very disturbing or indoctrinating material. There are provisions regarding films (e.g. PG, 15 or 18 certificates) and entry into sex shops. The fact, however, remains that quite a lot of censorship goes on in books for older children rather at the whim of the publisher and sometimes unknown to the author. An excellent article in *Children's Literature in Education*[1] by Jessica Yates provides some very useful information on this subject, particularly in relation to books for older children. At one time, books on sex for children or lessons on the subject in schools were minimal. Lessons were confined to odd token talks which were not very helpful or informative and books were more or less non-existent. This, of course, has changed tremendously in the last 15 to 20 years.

There remains, I feel, the idea that young children are better left in ignorance of sex as long as possible and they are not really interested anyway! Obviously, parents are the most suitable people to tell young children where babies come from and what is involved in sex relationships as boys and girls are individual and differ widely in their developmental needs. This does not mean, however, that they should be left in ignorance to obtain often disturbing and inaccurate information from their playmates or older children. Many parents are prejudiced against both telling their children or providing them with helpful and informative printed material about sex and nowadays there are many excellent books available for a variety of ages, often in picture book form. Nursery, Infant and Junior schools would be offering a very helpful service if a small library of such books could be available at school for parents to borrow.

Bookshops often do not appear to display picture or information books on sex, feeling no doubt that the general public would object and complain. If such a bias exists, and I have a strong feeling it does, then in the long run we are denying our children information they have a right to possess.

Many adults are seemingly unaware of young children's interest and curiosity about their own bodies and the harmless sex play

---

[1] *Children's Literature in Education*, Jessica Yates, Censorship in children's paperbacks, Winter 1980. Vol. II, pp. 181–191.

which goes on unnoticed. Children, too, sense that questions on the subject are unwelcomed and so keep silent.

Do adults have pre-conceived ideas about what older children need? Picture books, for example, tend to be associated with young children and as soon as boys and girls can read and reach the age of discretion, whenever that may be, picture books are 'out'. Information books on such subjects as volcanoes, birds' eggs, fossils, weapons of war and such things are permissible, but what we think of as genuine picture books are not.

Some picture books, of course, contain illustrations and tales which are too sophisticated for the very young and they can find no point of contact. Picture, story and child then have little to say to each other for here is an unfamiliar world. I have watched small boys and girls turning the pages of such books, looking for something that is meaningful for them at their stage of development – and finding nothing. Such books are dealing with emotions portrayed in such a way as to be beyond their grasp. Charles Keeping's *Through the Window* and *Joseph's Yard* (OUP) are both picture books which give older children glimpses into sudden death and the destroying despair of jealous and possessive love for which older boys and girls are emotionally ready.

What about comics? At one time these were frowned upon by adults. But they have always been enjoyed by children. Alas, their price today is beyond many children's means. Comic books, however, with a cartoon format appear to be doing very well, especially now that schools and libraries have accepted them. The Dr Seuss books with their controlled vocabulary and amusing pictures appealed to and helped the slow reader in school and perhaps started a vogue.

Comic books, I think, appeal to children for a variety of reasons; the actual reading material is short and the plot develops through the illustrations; what happens tends to mock at adult respectability (e.g. Raymond Briggs's *Father Xmas* and *Fungus the Bogeyman* published by Heinemann); and they possess a resilient, slapstick and robust quality which produces laughter and appeals so instinctively to children from about seven upwards.

Another development in the book world is the emergence of what some of us remember as the pop-up books – in a more elaborate form i.e. split page, peep show, hide and seek, pull down a flap, open a little door. I'm afraid I tend to think of these as somewhat 'gimmicky'. Boys and girls find them very intriguing with so many little attachments to manipulate. They tend, alas, to be somewhat fragile, generally contain a meagre story and their charm lies in the mechanics of the devices employed. Children's fingers tend to want to find out 'how it all works' and the books get broken. When I found *Alice's Adventures in Wonderland* and *Alice Through the Looking Glass* in pop-up form, my heart sank. It seems such a pity to see such 'classics' abridged and presented in pop-up form. They should be left in their original form to be appreciated and understood by older children – for whom they were written.

Finally, do we think of books as being 'boys' books' and 'girls' books', as we tend to think of toys (i.e. dolls for girls and engines for boys)? Most books and toys appeal to both sexes and it is adult suggestion from a very early age which tends to underline differences between the sexes, rather than their similarities.

It is not, therefore, an easy task when we are deciding what story and picture books children are going to enjoy. We need either as authors, artists, publishers or parents to understand young children's developmental needs and the emotional and intellectual stages they are passing through, if books are going to become a real part of their lives and an everlasting joy.

10
Conclusions

Snip, snap, snout,
This tale's told out.

In the preceding chapters I have tried to show the importance of early picture books, stories and poetry in the lives of young children and the part we as adults need to play.

Ezra Pound, in his *A.B.C. of Reading* says, 'Gloom and solemnity are entirely out of place in even the most rigorous study of an art originally intended to make glad the heart of man' and this, surely, is particularly true in relation to children, for books are for joy and gladness.

Perhaps when boys and girls grow up they may not find reading pleasurable. They may be rather poor and slow readers and prefer to get their stories and drama from watching television, films and plays, or from listening to the radio. Perhaps real life is so full of work or so dramatic and exciting that nothing else is needed. At the preschool and infant school stage, however, it would be difficult to find a child who did not enjoy listening to stories and poetry and looking at picture books.

By their early enjoyment, even at this stage, without realizing it, children will, perhaps unconsciously, acquire certain fundamental feelings in regard to literature and life. They will, unknowingly, accept the fact of the universality of human emotion, for imaginatively and through identification in fantasy in their picture books, stories and poetry they will share the feelings and needs of others. They will be given words, even if only in a limited degree, with which to express themselves, and they will hear how language can be used by others in a rich, exciting and moving way. They will know, too, that between the covers of books all sorts of wonderful things do happen and that they can find, if they so wish, the accumulated knowledge and wisdom of humankind with its mistakes, miseries, hopes, joys and fears, its horror and its glory. They will have been able to compensate themselves in some measure for the things life has denied them and to relive vicariously experiences that they cannot have in reality. Through looking at pictures, their horizons will be stretched far beyond their own four walls, and people, places and things all over the world will become theirs.

As children become older, early experiences will no doubt slip away from them; lost in seeming oblivion. I am quite sure, however, that that which is of value to personal growth and development, remains somewhere as a part of them – it is neither wasted nor lost, just as the bad things remain too. Everything that happens in life leaves its mark for good or ill. We want children to build up a store of satisfying and enriching experiences so that they will have something on which to draw as life goes on.

Books, like all real things in life, are meant to be used and not kept just for special occasions. 'No book', says John Ruskin in *Sesame and Lilies*, 'is worth anything which is not worth much; nor is it serviceable until it has been read and reread and loved and loved again.' Children certainly show with affectionate delight their feelings about their favourite books, which often fall to pieces with continued use.

Children will find amongst the books they enjoy many that deal mainly with facts, books of information concerned with such things as pond life, stars, railways, plants, numbers and a host of other topics. Such books are a useful addition to any child's collection and factual knowledge can give boys and girls a feeling of security; the known is less frightening than the unknown.

It is possible to escape into a factual world and avoid the world of feeling. It is not enough to know how something works, how to make a new machine, a new drug, a new instrument, we must feel the desire to develop it and use it for the good of humankind. A whole book could be written on the general intellectual interests of children under eight, how such material should be presented, written and illustrated and linked with their day to day lives. I have chosen here, however, to deal only with imaginative literature, with stories and poetry which will, in their own way, teach children about the art of living.

Some Practical Points

1. Young children can be helped to cherish and take care of books:
   (a) By example – by the way in which we ourselves use them.
   (b) By learning to treat books carefully – to have clean hands to turn over the pages correctly; not to tear or scribble on them.
2. Never give children books that are torn, dirty, dog-eared, as such books will only encourage careless treatment.
3. Children should have books of their own with a place to keep them, so that they think of them as treasured possessions.
4. Children should have plenty of play materials such as clay, water, sand, paint, etc., for vigorous, aggressive play so that they will not work out their angry, destructive feelings on their books.
5. Books should be suitably displayed, in generous supply and easy to get at in school so that children will enjoy using and finding those they want.
6. Never allow the beginnings of learning to read to be associated with unhappiness, fear or a sense of failure. These feelings can easily arise if children are made to learn to read before they are ready.
7. Never attempt to censor children's reading; this, in any case, is impossible – they will outwit us every time. Remember that we must take the blame if boys and girls continually choose the shoddy and the second-rate.
8. Children should be encouraged to use their public libraries.

Some reminders in the choosing of books for children:

PLOT
Does the book tell a good story?
Is it one that is possible to believe in at either the imaginative or the reality level?
Is there action and suspense however simple?
Is it plausible and credible without relying on coincidence and contrivance?

Content and Theme

Is the story appropriate for the age and the stage of development for which it has been designed?

Is the story worth telling?

Does it avoid moralizing and yet help to give children a sense of values and purpose?

Do truth and justice prevail?

Characterization

Are the characters real and convincing?

Can one see both their strengths and their weaknesses, particularly in the story for the older child who can see people as not either wholly good or wholly bad?

Has the author avoided types?

Do the characters develop and grow?

Style

Does the style fit the story and the subject matter?

Is it clear and understandable, with dialogue suitable to the characters?

Is there an exciting and imaginative use of words and a richness of expression?

Format

Is the appearance of the book attractive?

Is it durable, with print appropriate to the age for which it is planned and paper of good quality?

Do the illustrations add to its attraction, echoing and enhancing the story and stimulating children's imaginations and curiosity?

If it is meant to provide children with real information is it accurate in text and illustration?

Five Stories to Tell

Aloysius the Redundant Engine

Aloysius the Engine puffed slowly into the station at Little Scuffington and stopped. Jim O'Harrity looked out from his cabin, glancing up and down the almost empty platform.

'Well, well, that's the end, I suppose,' he said sadly to Jeremiah Jones the station master who came towards him holding his green flag under his arm. 'We may as well go home and dig our gardens and lock up the station. No more trains will ever stop here. I'll just drive Aloysius up the line beyond the platform and leave him. It's a sad day for Little Scuffington and no mistake.'

Jim O'Harrity looked at the large notice pinned to the wall which read: STATION PERMANENTLY CLOSED.

'I'll give you a final send off,' said Jeremiah Jones and he waved his green flag and blew a shrill blast on his whistle. Jim O'Harrity got up steam and drove Aloysius to where the line ended.

It was a lonely, quiet place. A stream ran down the hillside below the line and on through the sandhills to a pebbly beach and then on to the sea.

'I'm redundant,' said Aloysius to himself sadly. 'No one wants me. I'm no use any more, that's what being redundant means.'

He knew he was not very beautiful or up to date. His one long carriage was very shabby and his little buffet with its counter and shelves was badly in need of a fresh coat of paint. Still they had always been clean and tidy and Aloysius knew he had never had an accident or been more than two minutes late. It was not his fault that Little Scuffington station had been closed down for ever and a large, red, conceited bus had taken his place. So, at the end of the line where nobody would notice him, Aloysius settled down to his lonely and rather melancholy life.

The summer months passed and Aloysius know his joints were getting stiff and his paint was scruffy. The leaves on the trees turned from green to gold, hazel nuts ripened and the blackberries grew big and juicy.

Winter brought frosty mornings and cold winds. The stream which had run so quietly under the railway line in summer, became full of dark, swiftly-flowing water. One night there was a terrific storm. There was thunder and lightning. The wind blew in great fierce gusts. The water in the stream overflowed its banks and rose higher and higher until it was rushing and swirling right beneath Aloysius's wheels. He was surrounded by water.

Then all at once, without a second's warning, the ground beneath him began to shift and move as the water swept the earth and grass away from beneath his wheels. Before Aloysius knew what was happening he found himself being swept towards the beach and the sea. With the sound of breaking branches, falling stones and sliding earth, Aloysius and his carriage and buffet were swept along. He landed with a terrific bump in a hollow in the sandhills. The roaring of the waves on the pebbly beach sounded very close. Aloysius felt extremely frightened and shaken. He felt even more deserted and alone than before. He could just see in the half-light a monstrous stretch of grey-green, heaving water stretching as far as the sky.

Little did Aloysius know, however, that his days of loneliness were almost over and he was going to lead a happy and useful life again.

Just near him on the beach, Mr and Mrs Patrick O'Donigan had been living with their family in two large orange tents. They had left their own cottage among the hills when it had fallen to pieces around them. As they had no place to go they settled themselves, with all their worldly possessions, on the beach.

There was Mr and Mrs Patrick O'Donigan, old Uncle Enoch, Harry and James the twins, little Victoria Louise, Pinky Poll the baby, Bertie the dog, Hyacinth the cat and Twinkle Toes the parrot.

They had been sleeping peacefully on their camp beds when suddenly a terrific gust of wind picked their tents up and took them out to sea. It dropped them tidily beneath the waves, before tearing off to do some more damage.

Mr and Mrs Patrick O'Donigan awoke with a start; Uncle Enoch fell out of bed; Harry and James the twins began to bawl; little Victoria Louise screamed at the top of her voice; Pinky Poll the baby laughed like anything; Bertie the dog tried to dig a hole in the sand; Hyacinth the cat rushed for the nearest tree; and Twinkle Toes the parrot kept saying 'Oh what a beautiful morning' over and over again.

Mr and Mrs Patrick O'Donigan looked around helplessly at the heaving sea and the scudding clouds, the wet mist and the rain. What could they do?

Then looming out of the mist they saw a huge black shape in a hollow in the sandhills. What could it be? Some monster from the deep!

Uncle Enoch waded over to investigate. 'Saved,' he shouted. 'Saved. Shelter from the storm, all home comforts, free bed and lodging, a roof over our heads, a home at last.' For there was Aloysius – his carriage doors wide open, looking strong, solid, weatherproof and homely.

The family threw themselves and their belongings inside. There was a jumble of bodies, blankets, saucepans, tinned food, clothes, knives and forks, buckets and jam jars and hundreds of other things. It was a terrible mess but they were out of the storm. They settled down to sleep, warm and safe.

When morning came the storm had died down. A watery sun appeared, the wind dropped and the sea looked flat and grey but not nearly so angry.

Uncle Enoch started getting breakfast and soon a wonderful smell of bacon, coffee and burnt toast issued from Aloysius's buffet. There was just room for everyone to sit along the bar in the buffet. 'Just like old times,' thought Aloysius happily.

Then Mr and Mrs Patrick O'Donigan began sorting out beds and clothes, blankets and kitchen utensils. They began finding a place for everything and Aloysius felt more and more delighted.

In a few weeks' time you would not have known him. He was clean and polished with curtains at the window. Solidly settled in the hollow, not too close to the sea but able to enjoy the sight and sound of the waves rippling on the sand. There was a neat little fence round him to provide a feeling of privacy and a place for the children to play. Aloysius knew he was a happy engine again.

'Oh how lucky I am,' he murmured happily.

So the family settled down. The children went to school. Uncle Enoch did the cooking. Mr O'Donigan got a job collecting fares on the large, red, conceited bus. Mrs O'Donigan kept the place clean and tidy, collected shells and went beachcombing after every high tide.

AND AS FAR AS I KNOW THEY ARE LIVING THERE STILL.

The No Good Cats

Slippery Sal was a No Good cat. Everyone said she was no good, so she knew she must be. She was black and slinky, with a stringy tail, green eyes and sharp, white teeth. She had no home and no friends. She slept among old garbage cans and on rubbish dumps, in deserted gardens and empty woodsheds.

On fine nights, when the moon sailed proudly across the purple, dark sky, Slippery Sal sat on the tiles and howled mournfully to the distant stars. The windows of all the elegant and expensive houses round about would open, doors would be slammed loudly and people would shout angrily: 'There's that No Good cat again. Can't we get rid of her!'

Even the other cats in the neighbourhood were too proud and haughty to speak to Slippery Sal. Most of them were chinchillas, silver tabbies or blue persians; their necks were bedecked with medals. If they saw Slippery Sal slinking across the road or sneaking past the window, they would mew indignantly: 'There goes that No Good cat again. Let's chase her away.'

Slippery Sal was always hungry, for food was not easy to find. She crept through half-open pantry windows, or squeezed past half-closed kitchen doors, and took whatever she could find: left-over scraps, bits of chicken pie, cold potatoes, mouldy bread.

One evening Slippery Sal was feeling particularly dejected. She had been wandering about for hours and all she had found were some tough old bones put out for the dogs. Suddenly, crossing the garden of a palatial house, she came upon a half-open back door. Creeping silently inside, she found herself in a big, warm kitchen. In front of the fire was a bowl of milk. Lying on a rug was an ugly, white kitten with blue eyes and a black-tipped nose.

Slippery Sal was just preparing to pounce on the kitten and give it a sharp nip with her teeth, when the kitten suddenly looked up.

'Oh please,' the kitten mewed pitifully, 'don't hurt me. I'm just an ugly little No Good kitten, but I've never done anyone any harm.'

'What!' said Slippery Sal, pulling herself up with a jerk. 'A No Good kitten – how come? I'm a No Good cat.'

'Oh I'm so ordinary,' said the kitten sadly, 'everyone calls me Pussy Plain. My mother and sisters are the most beautiful white persians. No one knows what happened to me, but I'm going to run away and I know just where I shall go.'

Slippery Sal scratched one ear with her paw, flicked her long, stringy tail. 'Let's run away together,' she said. 'If you're a No Good kitten and I'm a No Good cat we ought to stick with each other.'

'We'll go this very evening,' said Pussy Plain determinedly. 'I have a great aunt called Clotilda Cream. She lives on the other side of town. She will advise us.'

So Slippery Sal and Pussy Plain stole out of the house together; Pussy Plain leading the way. They padded down the deserted road; through the empty park; across the railway lines; under the arched bridge; and along by the slow moving river. It was a long way but at last they came to a street full of small houses with little back gardens.

'This is Geranium Row. My great aunt Clotilda Cream lives at number 7,' said Pussy Plain.

On the back wall of number 7 great aunt Clotilda Cream sat gossiping with several of her cat friends. She was a large, majestic ginger cat with a sweeping tail. She welcomed Pussy Plain joyfully.

'Well, well,' she mewed, 'I wondered when you were going to leave those stuck-up relatives of yours. I see you've brought a friend with you.'

'Please great aunt Clotilda Cream,' said Pussy Plain. 'Do find us a nice home with someone who will really love us. We are so tired of being No Good cats.'

'I know just the place,' said Tiger Boy, a sleek, grizzled tom with long whiskers and yellow eyes. 'Mrs Green at number 12 lives all alone a lot of the time, her husband goes to sea. She would love two nice cats to catch the mice in her cellar and sit in front of the fire and purr on winter evenings. Go and scratch on her door, she will be sure to take you in.'

Slippery Sal and Pussy Plain hurried along and scratched on the door of number 12. They were tired and hungry. It had begun to rain. Mrs Eliza Green opened the door.

'My gracious,' she said. 'Two poor little cats out on a miserable night like this. Come in.' She picked up Pussy Plain under one arm and Slippery Sal under the other. Then she took them into her lovely warm kitchen. There was a thick hearth rug and comfortable chairs. 'Now you sit by the fire and I'll get you a bite of supper,' she said. 'I've been wanting a nice cat to keep me company and get rid of the mice. It will be even better to have two cats instead of one.'

Slippery Sal and Pussy Plain settled down to a tasty supper. They felt very welcomed.

'Well, you are beautiful cats,' said Mrs Eliza Green. 'I can see you will do me credit.'

Slippery Sal began to wash her face and wash behind her ears with great thoroughness. Pussy Plain started to wash her tail. They were both rather dirty and bedraggled.

From that moment Slippery Sal and Pussy Plain began to grow into plump, happy, well-behaved, kind, lovable cats. Slippery Sal stayed in at night and she and Pussy Plain slept on soft cushions in the kitchen. They kept Mrs Eliza Green's house free of mice. As for being No Good cats, well no one ever mentioned the word, and anyway Slippery Sal and Pussy Plain were Good cats – now!

Mr Jones Buys a Ladder

Mr and Mrs Jones lived at number 6 Cherry Tree Road. They had a nice little house with a green door, a little garden at the front and quite a big garden at the back. Mr Jones had a toolshed at the bottom of the back garden and in it he had a lawnmower, a spade, a rake, a wheelbarrow, a fork and a pair of shears. But what Mr Jones wanted more than anything else was a ladder – a nice, long ladder.

One Saturday afternoon he walked up to the corner shop, which sold all sorts of things, to buy a ball of string. There, standing up in a corner, was a magnificent ladder. It was painted scarlet and Mr Jones knew that if he bought it he would be able to use it to reach the top bedroom window which needed mending and to pick all his apples and plums – even those that grew at the very tops of the trees.

Mr Jones felt very pleased. He hurried home to get some money. Very soon he was back in the shop to buy the long, scarlet ladder. It was rather heavy to carry and he had to walk very slowly down

Cherry Tree Road. At last he got it safely home.

Now everyone who lived in Cherry Tree Road was very interested to see Mr Jones coming home with such a smart, scarlet ladder. He left it leaning against his garden wall while he went into the house to have a cup of tea. All the time, he was thinking of the things he would be able to do with his new scarlet ladder.

He had just drunk his first cup of tea when there was a loud rat-tat on the door. Outside were Peter and Alice from next door.

'Please Mr Jones,' said Alice. 'Could you help us? We saw you bring that lovely, bright, scarlet ladder home and our kitten has climbed up on to a high branch on the apple tree and she can't get down. Will you please bring your ladder and save her for us?'

'Oh dear,' said Mr Jones with a sigh, but he got up and went outside. He carried his new scarlet ladder into the next door garden and rested it against the apple tree. Then he climbed up very carefully and brought the kitten down safely.

'Oh thank you,' said Peter and Alice.

Mr Jones took the ladder back into his garden and went inside to finish his tea.

He had just sat down, with a large curranty slice of home-made cake on his plate, when there was a loud rat-tat-tat at the door. Outside was Mrs Smith who lived across the road.

'Oh please, Mr Jones,' she said, 'I saw you bring that lovely, enormous, scarlet ladder home. Can you help me? My Billy has climbed out of his bedroom window and now he can't get back or down. Will you please bring your ladder and save him from certain death?'

'Tiresome child,' thought Mr Jones, but he got up and went outside. He took his scarlet ladder across the road, rested it against the side of the house, climbed up carefully and brought Billy down. 'And don't do such a silly thing again,' he said crossly.

'Oh thank you!' said Mrs Smith.

Mr Jones took the ladder back to his own garden and went inside to have a second cup of tea. He had just sat down, with a large chocolate biscuit on his plate, when there was a loud rat-tat-tat on the door. Outside were Mr and Mrs Green and their three children.

'Oh please, Mr Jones, could you help us? We hear you have

bought a superb new scarlet ladder. We have been out for the day and we've left the doorkey on the kitchen table. There is a window open upstairs and if we could borrow your superb new ladder, one of us could climb up, get through the window, retrieve the key and open the door.'

'Oh dear, oh dear, a very foolish thing to do,' said Mr Jones. 'You should never leave windows open when you got out, or forget doorkeys.' However, he got up and with the help of the ladder Mr Green climbed up, got into the house, opened the front door, and let Mrs Green and the children into the house.

'Oh thank you so much,' said Mr and Mrs Green and all the children together. Mr Jones took his ladder back into his own garden and went indoors.

'I'm going to take the dog out for a walk,' he said to his wife. 'There are a lot more people living in Cherry Tree Road and I shouldn't be surprised if they all come along soon and want to borrow my ladder.'

'It's very nice to be able to help people,' said Mrs Jones.

Mr Jones went out with the dog and Mrs Jones made an apple pie for supper. Everyone in Cherry Tree Road must have seen Mr Jones go out, for no one else came along to borrow his ladder.

The Mary Jane

Once upon a time there was a little boat called the *Mary Jane*. She was not a very big boat and she did not live at the seaside, but by a river. She was tied up to a small jetty way out in the country. Quite often she was used to ferry children and their parents to the other side of the river to pick buttercups and daisies or to picnic in the meadows.

The water in the little river was a lovely deep green. Sometimes it was so clear the fish could be seen darting in and out among the waterweeds. Sometimes the wind blew the water and it became full of soft, dark shadows.

The *Mary Jane* was a happy little boat, and she liked her home. She liked taking the children to play in the fields and she liked bringing them back with their hands full of flowers. One morning when the *Mary Jane* woke up, she was not alone. At the jetty, tied up beside her, was a large motorboat looking very smart. She was painted white with lots of shining brass and a red and yellow flag fluttering from her mast. She looked very proud and haughty.

When she saw the *Mary Jane* was looking, the motorboat said in a deep, loud voice, 'What a dreadfully quiet place this is! I simply could not sleep last night.'

The *Mary Jane* looked a little surprised. 'It is very quiet,' she said, 'but that makes it so peaceful.'

'Oh dear me no,' said the motorboat in a deep, loud voice. 'Where I live it is very exciting and lively. I live in the town harbour. There's a railway station, a jetty for steamers and a jetty for big boats to take on loads of coal and all sorts of goods. There are shops and motor cars and crowds of people. We have enormous ships at our jetty.'

'We have beautiful white swans,' said the *Mary Jane*.

'You should see our big red buses,' said the motorboat proudly.

'Our fields are full of buttercups and daisies,' said the *Mary Jane*.

'We have crowds and crowds of people,' said the motorboat.

'We have a few little ducks,' said the *Mary Jane* with a sigh. 'But I would like to visit the town. Is it a long way?'

'Yes,' said the motorboat. 'It is a long way but I have an engine so I came up quickly. It would take a little boat like you much longer.'

The *Mary Jane* felt a little sad.

'If you would really like to leave this depressing place,' said the motorboat, 'I think it could be managed. When it gets dark I will give you a big push. You are not fastened to the jetty very securely, your rope will slip and then the river will take you down to the sea.'

'That would be most exciting,' said the *Mary Jane*.

That night it was very dark indeed and when the church clock struck 12 the motorboat gave the *Mary Jane* a mighty push. Her rope slipped and in a moment she was free, floating quietly and swiftly down the river to the sea.

All night long the *Mary Jane* moved steadily on and on. When morning came she was a long way from home. Everything looked very strange. The riverbanks were high and steep. The water ran so quickly that the *Mary Jane* began to feel a little frightened. Then, suddenly, right in front of her and coming very, very fast was an enormous boat. It was full of people talking and laughing. As it pushed its way through the water it made big, white, crested waves.

'Oh dear, what shall I do?' said the *Mary Jane* in a frightened whisper. 'I shall be swamped!'

A wave splashed against her sides and another and another. Then suddenly a very large wave lifted her up into the air and tossed her into a bed of thick reeds. With a surge and a rush the big boat had gone. Slowly the waves died away into little ripples.

'Oh dear. What an adventure!' said the *Mary Jane* in a very breathless voice. She felt very tired and very bruised as she lay among the reeds.

A large brown duck came swimming by. 'Quack, quack,' said the duck. 'What's this? Oh, only a little boat!' And off went the duck with her tail in the air.

A beautiful white swan came sailing by but she never even saw the little boat.

The *Mary Jane* was so pleased, however, to be lying quietly on her bed of reeds, she did not care what happened to her, at that moment. 'I shall stay for the night. I shall have a rest,' she said to herself. 'And when the sun rises again perhaps I will go off on my travels to the sea.'

So she went to sleep. Very soon it got dark. The stars came out and the moon made a soft, silver path on the water. Everything was very still.

Morning came and the *Mary Jane* who had been sleeping on her bed of reeds all night, woke up. She felt better after her long sleep and was all ready to set off on her journey again.

Then she found out that there was not enough water for her to float in and she was high and dry in her bed of reeds. 'Oh dear, will I have to stay here for the rest of my life?' said the *Mary Jane*. There was no one about to ask for help. It began to get hot. A light wind ruffled the water and the reeds made a soft, shivering sound.

'Don't worry little boat,' the reeds seemed to say. 'In a little while the tide will come in very gently. Then there will be just enough water to float in and the tide is so quiet you will float slowly down to the sea.'

Gradually the water began to rise very gently and very calmly. Soon there was enough to float the *Mary Jane* off her bed of reeds and take her peacefully into the middle of the river so that she began to float once more serenely down towards the sea.

'I'm beginning my adventures again,' said the *Mary Jane*. 'I wonder what will happen now?'

The *Mary Jane* floated on and presently the river began to get wider. Instead of the green fields and tall trees on either side, there were houses and factories with tall chimneys. Then the *Mary Jane* floated under a bridge. She saw buses and cars and lots and lots of people, just as the motorboat had said. Then the river suddenly seemed to be full of boats. There were big boats and little boats, some with white sails, some with brown sails. There were seagulls skimming over the tops of the waves. The sky was blue, but the water was a strange browny-green with curly white waves.

'This must be the sea!' said the *Mary Jane*.

The waves began to get quite big. They took the *Mary Jane* and bumped her against the sides of the other boats who all looked very annoyed. They were all anchored, but the *Mary Jane* had nothing to hold her and she went dancing over the water like a cork. Presently she had left all the other boats behind and was out in the middle of the sea, all by herself.

The *Mary Jane* began to feel very lonely and scared. There was no one to talk to and nothing to see but the browny-green water and white-capped waves. She wondered whatever was going to happen to her.

'Perhaps,' thought the *Mary Jane*, 'I shall go on sailing and sailing and never, never stop until I come to the end of the world.'

It began to get cold. The sun was sinking. Soon it would be dark.

'Oh dear! Why did I leave my safe little jetty?' moaned the *Mary Jane*. 'I wonder what all the children are doing without me? They will have no one to take them across the river to picnic and to pick buttercups and daisies.' She felt very, very unhappy and terribly frightened.

Then suddenly out of the shadows there loomed a white and silver shape. It was a large motorboat. It was the very same one that the *Mary Jane* had talked to when she had stopped near her jetty.

'What are *you* doing?' said the motorboat who was safely anchored. 'You're a very long way from home.'

'I'm lost,' said the *Mary Jane*. 'I shall never see my dear little jetty again or the children I ferry across to the green meadows.'

'Cheer up,' said the motorboat. 'I can easily save you. Catch hold.' The motorboat threw the *Mary Jane* a rope. 'Now I'll cast anchor. I've nothing to do at the moment and in no time I'll have you home. Just hang on.'

It was quite dark by this time and the sky was full of stars. The rope was secure round one of the *Mary Jane*'s seats. The motorboat chugged on going swiftly and steadily on and on. It seemed a long way but the *Mary Jane* didn't mind a bit. She felt so happy.

Then at last the *Mary Jane* was home, tied up alongside her own little jetty. 'Goodbye,' said the motorboat. 'I shall go now; you are safe and happy again. Don't go roaming again, little boat.'

'I shan't,' said the *Mary Jane*. 'Thank you, thank you. I'm so grateful for your help.'

'You're welcome,' said the motorboat and it chugged off into the darkness.

The Little Blue Door

Betsy Lou lived in a tall, narrow house. She had a little attic bedroom with a sloping ceiling. Through the window she could see grey roofs, smoking chimneys, neat little gardens and stretches of sky.

In one corner of her room there was a little blue door. It had been locked ever since Betsy Lou could remember. The key had been lost years and years ago.

One afternoon Betsy Lou was feeling very lonely because she had no one to play with. It was then that she found a box in her doll's house. In the small box was a tiny, tiny, rusty key. It looked as if it would fit a very small door. Betsy Lou thought she would see if it would open the little blue door in her bedroom. It did – it fitted it exactly. Betsy Lou turned the key gently and the little blue door creaked slowly open. She heard a sound like the sighing of wind over water and smelled the dry, dusty scent of lavender, cobwebs and old books. She found herself in a dark, narrow room packed with all kinds of mysterious things: toys of all sorts, piles of tattered books, old bits of furniture and bundles of papers tied up with string.

Betsy Lou stood inside the room and looked round. There was a square window covered with cobwebs in the sloping roof. Suddenly out of the dusky shadows a mournful voice spoke: 'What are you doing here?' Sitting in the corner in a large rocking chair was a small stuffed giraffe.

'We haven't had any visitors for years and years and years,' said a musical box. 'Now you're here, please wind me up. I haven't heard my own tunes for such a long time.'

'Oh do please put me together again,' murmured a puzzle. 'I'm in pieces and I feel all broken up. When I'm put together you will see a lovely picture of the seaside.'

'Tuck me up and rock me to sleep,' wailed a baby doll in a wooden cradle. 'I'm so tired, so very, very tired.'

'You could build a magnificent castle or house, or railway station,' said a large box of bricks.

Betsy Lou looked round. There were so many things to see and so many things to do, she didn't know where to begin. All the toys seemed to want to have something done.

Hanging on the door, Betsy Lou saw a beautiful, poppy scarlet cloak, a hat with a sweeping feather and a long, golden silk scarf. Clothes that a princess would wear. Betsy Lou loved dressing up and here were such wonderful clothes.

'Oh I must put them on before I do anything else,' she said.

She took the poppy scarlet cloak and the hat and put them on. She tugged at the golden silk scarf. It would not come off. She tugged again and again. It just would not come off the hook. The attic door creaked as she pulled.

'Be careful. Be very, very careful,' mewed a purple velvet cat from beside a pile of papers.

'Oh do think what you are doing,' squeaked a clockwork mouse.

'I can't warn you in time!' moaned a grandfather's clock. 'My works are all run down.'

'Beware, beware,' whispered a picture book, fluttering its pages frantically.

Betsy Lou took no notice. She just went on tugging and tugging at the long, golden silk scarf. She did not even listen. All she wanted was to look like a princess.

All at once it happened. The little blue door creaked and began to move very, very slowly. Then it closed with a click. The key was on the other side. She was locked in.

'Now look what you have done, you foolish child!' shouted the stuffed giraffe.

101

At first Betsy Lou did not realize what had happened. Then she became very frightened. She was locked in!

'Oh, what shall I do!' she cried. She tried to open the door but it would not move.

'No one will know where I am,' she sobbed. 'Perhaps I shall stay here for ever and ever, like all the toys.'

'We warned you,' said the purple velvet cat and the clockwork mouse. 'We know what it is like to be locked in for years and years and years!'

'You never wound me up,' sighed the musical box in a sad voice.

'You didn't rock me to sleep,' wailed a baby doll. 'And I was so very, very tired.'

'You took no notice of us at all. We might not have been here!' shouted the puzzle and the bricks in furious voices.

'She is a selfish and careless child,' muttered the giraffe.

'Yes,' sighed all the toys. 'She is a selfish and careless child. Now she is a prisoner like us. Perhaps she will have to stay here, locked up for hundreds and hundreds of years.'

'I'm sorry, I'm really sorry,' wept Betsy Lou. 'I didn't think. I just wanted to be a princess.'

'She didn't think. She didn't think,' murmured the toys.

Suddenly everyone stopped talking and it became very, very quiet. Gradually the little room became dim and shadowy as the sun went down. Betsy Lou sat on a broken stool and pulled the poppy scarlet cloak around her shoulders. It was getting cold.

Then a tinny voice spoke to her from out of the shadows. 'I think perhaps I can help you,' said the tinny voice. 'Lift up my lid and look inside.' The voice came from an old rusty moneybox on the floor. Betsy Lou stooped down and raised the lid. Inside was a tiny key. She picked it up and put it into the lock on the door. It fitted exactly. She turned it slowly and carefully. The door creaked gently open. Betsy Lou stepped outside.

She was back again in her own little room. She had no time to say goodbye to the toys but she heard a sorrowful sigh as the little blue door closed behind her. She still had her poppy scarlet cloak round her shoulders.

Then she heard her mother's voice calling her to tea.

'Where have you been?' asked her mother. 'What a lovely poppy scarlet cloak you are wearing.'

Betsy Lou told her mother all about the little blue door and all the toys locked up in the attic.

'I think we will have to explore it together,' said her mother. 'Those toys need to be played with.'

Betsy Lou sighed with happiness. Now the toys will be happy again.

Bibliography

There are certain picture books for the very young and story books for the older child that one feels should be part of every boy and girl's reading life. It is not that we are going to demand that such books should be read, but because they are a part of the world's literary heritage and contain much that children will delight in and enjoy, it would be tragic if they grew up not knowing of their existence. I have tried to include some of these.

Everyone will want to add to this list – favourites of their own, books which have meant a great deal to them and which they would like their children to enjoy – and, of course, many books come and go, they serve their purpose and vanish into limbo.

Most of the books in this list have stood the test of time because they possess a universal appeal, and amongst the somewhat bewildering collection of new books that are always appearing it is useful to have a few that one can hold on to as to a sheet anchor.

Whatever we may think, children change very little. They appear more sophisticated, their interests are perhaps wider as they take journeys into space for granted and air travel as a matter of course, accepted without question. Yet they have the same needs and problems, fears and pleasures, as we did.

Nothing can really take the place of books in our lives. We may talk about computers, tape recorders, radio, TV and who knows what new invention is round the corner, but the printed word, the world of stories and pictures, will not become obsolete for a very, very long time.

All children should hear stories about historical and legendary heroes and heroines, for example King Arthur, Robin Hood, Beowulf, Saint George; fairy stories from Grimm and Hans Andersen, Perrault and the Arabian Nights; and the myths and legends of the Greek, the Romans and the Norsemen. There are many collections of fairy stories and folk tales from England, Scotland, Ireland, Wales, Russia, Japan etc., available in a variety of different editions, and children enjoy these tales immensely.

The longer books that we think of as 'The Classics' (all obtainable in paperback) have not been mentioned here. There are so many of them and they are so easy to obtain from libraries and bookshops, in many different editions, it seemed unnecessary. Many children of 7 and 8 will enjoy stories such as *Black Beauty* (Anna Sewell), *The Just So Stories* (Rudyard Kipling), *Winnie the Pooh* (A. A. Milne), and *The Wind in the Willows* (Kenneth Grahame). Some boys and girls will need these books read aloud to them; the fluent and avid readers will read them easily themselves.

Some of the more modern writers – for example, P. L. Travers, Noel Streatfield, Mary Norton, Frances Hodgson Burnett, J. R. Tolkein – will be seized on by children. If you have missed out on them as a child and now read them aloud to your family or school class, you will enjoy them as much as the children.

1 Picture Books and Stories
There is no frigate like a book to take us lands away.
Emily Dickinson

ADAMSON, JEAN and GARETH. *Topsy and Tim's Monday Book*. Blackie.
There is a series of these books with simple, colourful pictures about everyday happenings – much enjoyed by children.

AHLBERG, JANET and ALLAN. *The Baby's Catalogue, Each Peach Pear and Plum*. Kestrel.
Just two of the charming and original picture books by Janet and Allan Ahlberg which have an irresistible appeal to children.

ARDIZZONE, EDWARD. *Little Tim and the Brave Sea Captain*. OUP.
There are a number of picture books about Little Tim and Charlotte as well as other picture story books with dramatic stories and exciting pictures by Edward Ardizzone.

AUSTIN, MARGOT. *Peter Churchmouse*. World's Work.
A very endearing mouse. There are several more books about him.

BANNERMAN, HELEN. *The Story of Little Black Sambo*. Chatto and Windus.
A tale dearly loved by children about a little boy's exciting

adventures with tigers and pancakes.

BEMELMANS, LUDWIG. *Madeline*. André Deutsch.
A rhyming story with a Parisian background; also *Madeline's Rescue, Madeline and the Bad Hat* – all about the same little girl and her adventures.

BERESTAIN, STAN and JAN. *The Berenstain Bear's New Baby*. Fontana Picture Lions.
A pleasing story about a new baby in the family. Lively cartoon pictures.

BIRO, VAL. *Gumdrop. The Adventures of a Vintage Car*. Hodder and Stoughton.
Just one among the many picture books about a vintage car. There are other picture story books, some in collaboration with H. E. Todd.

BLAKE, QUENTIN. *Patrick*. Puffin.
Patrick spends his last penny on a very special violin. Vivid and alive pictures by this gifted writer and illustrator.

BROOKE, LESLIE. *The Golden Goose Books*. Warne.
This series contains old favourites like The Three Bears, The Three Little Pigs etc. There are any number of these old tales retold and illustrated by different artists.

BRUNA, DICK. *The Little Bird*. Methuen.
Picture books by Dick Bruna – and there are a large number available – are very simple in content and picture for the very young.

BRUNHOFF, JEAN DE. *The Story of Babar, the Little Elephant*. Methuen.
This is just one among the many irresistible stories about the doings of Babar, written and illustrated by Jean de Brunhoff, which have been loved for so long. Jean de Brunhoff's son, Laurent, has continued the series and *That Rascal Arthur* is just one of the many titles available.

BURNINGHAM, JOHN. *Borka, The Adventures of a Goose with No Feathers*. Jonathan Cape.
There are all sorts of picture books written and illustrated by

John Burningham for a variety of tastes and ages. Borka finds safety and happiness when she lands in Kensington Gardens.

BURTON, VIRGINIA LEE. *The Little House*. Faber.
Katy and the Big Snow and *Mike Mulligan's Steam Shovel* are two other picture story books written and illustrated by this American author which are especially enjoyed by the 4–7 year olds.

CAMPBELL, ROD. *Dear Zoo*. Abelard.
One of the really charming books with little doors to open to show the pictures which illustrate the story.

CARLE, ERIC. *The Very Hungry Caterpillar*. Puffin.
A great favourite with children.

CASS, JOAN E. *Alexander's Magic Quilt, The Four Surprises*. Abelard.
Two picture books, illustrated by Tony Linsell, among a number of picture books for the 4–8 year olds by Joan Cass.

DUVOISIN, ROGER. *Petunia*. Bodley Head.
Petunia is an amusing goose. There are more picture books about Petunia, as well as a number of other delightful ones by this author/illustrator.

FATIO, LOUISE. *The Happy Lion*. Bodley Head.
Illustrated by Roger Duvoisin. One of those pleasurable picture books where a small boy proves himself cleverer than the grown ups. Set in a small French village. There are several more picture books about the happy lion and his friends, as well as a host of others.

FLACK, MARJORIE. *Angus and the Cat*. Bodley Head.
There are a series of simple picture books about Angus as well as Ping, the tale of a little duck on a boat on the Yangtze river (illustrated by Kurt Weise). No child should miss Ping – a truly endearing story.

FOREMAN, MICHAEL. *Horatio*. Puffin.
The story of a hippopotamus with an imagination.

GAG, WANDA. *Millions of Cats*. Faber.

A search for the prettiest cat in the world, written and illustrated by this American author. Enjoyed by young and old. Wanda Gag has written and illustrated other endearing books, but perhaps *Millions of Cats* is the best.

GRAMATKY, HARDIE. *Little Toot*. World's Work.
The story of a little tugboat who succeeds where all the other big boats have failed.

GRETZ, SUSANNA. *The Bears Who Stayed Indoors*. Puffin.
There is a series of picture books about these charming bears whose activities are endless. No one can help loving them.

HALE, KATHLEEN. *Orlando's Camping Holiday*. Methuen.
One of a number of old favourites about Orlando the Marmalade Cat and his wife Grace. Pictures full of fascinating detail.

HEWITT, ANITA. *The Tale of a Turnip*. Bodley Head.
Illustrated by Margery Gill. An old favourite retold.

HOBAN, RUSSELL and LILIAN. *A Baby Sister for Frances*. Faber.
There are a number of books about Frances, a little badger, and her family problems which are the kind of problems that children experience. There are many other picture books by these two gifted people.

HUGHES, SHIRLEY. *Lucy and Tom's Day*. Gollancz.
Shirley Hughes has written and illustrated a large number of attractive picture story books concerned with everyday events in which young children can share. She has written and illustrated a variety of story books, some for older children.

HUTCHINS, PAT. *The Surprise Party*. Bodley Head.
One of the many delightful books written and illustrated by Pat Hutchins.

KEATS, EZRA JACK. *The Snowy Day*. Bodley Head.
This American writer and illustrator has provided children with a number of delightful picture books concerned with their own day to day questioning – full of interesting incidents.

108

KEEPING, CHARLES. *Charley, Charlotte and the Golden Canary*. OUP.
Just one of the vividly illustrated books by Charles Keeping. It is
about the friendship between two children. Some of his picture
books are more suitable for children over 8.

KERR, JUDITH. *The Tiger Who Came to Tea*. Fontana Picture Lions.
I doubt if I would enjoy sitting down to tea with a tiger; however,
he appears to be an agreeable, if greedy creature.

KNASILOVSKY, PHYLLIS. *The Cow Who Fell in the Canal*. World's Work.
Illustrated by Peter Spier. A lovely Dutch setting for this un-
fortunate cow.

LOBEL, ARNOLD. *Prince Bertram the Bad*. Random House.
Comic pictures and a story to match.

MAYNE, WILLIAM. *The Patchwork Cat*. Cape.
Illustrated by Nicola Bayley. An exciting story with lovely
pictures. The author has written a number of books for older
children.

MCKEE, DAVID. *Two Can Toucan*. Abelard.
Just one of the laughter provoking stories and pictures by this
writer/illustrator.

PEPPE, RODNEY. *The Mice Who Lived in a Shoe*. Kestrel.

PIENKOWSKI, JAN. *Haunted House*. Heinemann.
One of this author/illustrator's pop-up books; funny and original.

POSTGATE, OLIVER. *Ivor the Engine*. Abelard-Schuman.
No one can resist the stories of Ivor the Welsh engine. He has the
most exciting adventures, but everything always turns out happily. Illustrated by Peter Firmin. There are other picture story
books by these two collaborators.

POTTER, BEATRIX. *The Tale of Peter Rabbit*. Warne.
The little books which Beatrix Potter wrote and illustrated are a
liberal education in themselves. They are listed here so that no
child should miss hearing and seeing a number of them: *The Tale
of Squirrel Nutkin, The Tale of Benjamin Bunny, The Tailor of
Gloucester, The Tale of Jeremy Fisher, The Tale of Tom Kitten, The*

Tale of the Two Bad Mice, The Tale of Mrs Tiggywinkle, The Tale of Mrs Tittlemouse, The Tale of Timmy Tiptoes, The Tale of Johnny Town Mouse, The Tale of Mr Toad, The Tale of Pigling Bland, The Tale of Samuel Whiskers, The Pie and the Patty Pan, The Tale of Little Pig Robinson, The Story of the Fierce Bad Rabbit, The Story of Mrs Moppet.

PROKOFIEV, SERGEI. *Peter and the Wolf.* Faber.
Illustrated by Alan Howard. There are a number of editions of this well-known commentary to Prokofiev's exciting music so one can take one's choice.

RETTICH, MARGARET. *The Voyage of the Jolly Boat.* Methuen.
English version by Olive Jones. An exciting story with lovely pictures.

ROSE, GERALD and ELIZABETH. *Old Winkle and the Seagulls.* Faber.
Old Winkle is kind to the seagulls and they guide him to where the fish are. Just one of the engaging books by Gerald and Elizabeth Rose.

ROSS, DIANA. *The Story of the Little Red Engine.* Faber.
Illustrated by Lewitt Him. There are a series of books about the little red engine and although they are not the huge diesels we see today children still find them very lovable.

ROSS, TONY. *Hugo and Odsock.* Transworld.
Cartoon like illustrations to an amusing story.

SCARRY, RICHARD. *Find Your ABC.* Fontana Picture Lions.
This is just one of the many picture books by this author/ illustrator. The pages are full of small lively pictures with brief information in between. Children find lots to look at and talk about.

SENDAK, MAURICE. *Where the Wild Things Are.* Puffin.
There are a number of other picture books by Maurice Sendak. Some with strange feelings and undertones in the text and illustration. They appeal to some children and adults, but not to others.

STOBBS, WILLIAM. *A Frog He Would A-Wooing Go*. Bodley Head.
Lovely pictures to an old tale. One of the many picture books by Williams Stobbs with illustrations one never tires of looking at.

TODD, H. E. *The Crawly, Crawly Caterpillar*. Carousel.
Illustrated by Val Biro. H. E. Todd has written a number of other stories children enjoy.

TITUS, EVA. *Anatole*. Puffin.
Illustrated by Paul Galdone. There are other stories about Anatole, an engaging little mouse.

UTTLEY, ALISON. *The Little Grey Rabbit Books*. Heinemann.
Also *The Little Red Fox Books*, *The Brown Mouse Books* – just a few of this writer's tales for children. Various illustrators.

VIPONT, ELFRIDA. *The Elephant and the Bad Baby*. Hamish Hamilton.
Illustrated by Raymond Briggs. Bad behaviour of either children or animals is always popular.

WELLINGTON, ANN. *Mr Bingley's Apple Pie*. Abelard.
Pictures by Nina Sowter. An amusing tale with warm, lively pictures.

WILDSMITH, BRIAN. *The Bear's Adventures*. OUP.
There are so many exciting picture books by Brian Wildsmith with lovely, lavish pictures to look at and look at again. One makes one's own choice. This is a recent publication.

WOOD, JOYCE. *Grandmother Lucy and Her Hats*. Fontana Picture Lions.
Illustrated by Frank Francis. Stories about kindly grandmothers are always loved by children and grandmother Lucy is no exception.

ZION, GENE. *Harry The Dirty Dog*. Puffin.
Illustrated by Margaret Bloy Graham. There are a number of books about Harry and his troubles. *The Plant Sitter* is another amusing story, when the plants Tommy is looking after grow to enormous sizes.

Many of the picture books on this list are available in paperback.

BOOKS WITH SHORT STORIES TO READ OR TELL

Just a very few of the many available for young children.

BERG, LEILA. *Little Pete Stories*. Puffin.
Leila Berg has written a number of stories and some collections of folk tales to tell and read to children. Useful collections for teachers and parents.

CRESSWELL, HELEN. *A Gift from Winklesea*. Puffin.
Just one of the many stories by Helen Cresswell much enjoyed by children.

COLWELL, EILEEN. *Tell me a Story, Tell Me Another Story, Time for a Story*. Puffin.
Very useful collections to use with children.

CORRIN, SARA and STEPHEN. *Stories for Under Fives*. Hamish Hamilton.
Illustrated by Shirley Hughes. Sara and Stephen Corrin have various other collections for a variety of different ages.

DAHL, ROALD. *Fantastic Mr Fox*. Puffin.
A story about a fox who liked helping himself to nice plump poultry. Just one of the many enjoyable tales by Roald Dahl.

DE LA MARE, WALTER. *Collected Stories for Children*. Faber.
A pleasing and varied collection.

DRUMMOND, J. H. *Mrs Easter's Parasol*. Faber.
Illustrated by the author. One in a series of longer story books for the 5–8 year olds.

EDWARDS, DOROTHY. *My Naughty Little Sister*. Methuen.
There are a number of stories and picture books about this bad little girl. Dorothy Edwards has also a number of collections of tales for reading aloud to the 5–7 year olds.

GODDEN, RUMER. *The Doll's House*. Puffin.
One of the many stories written by Rumer Godden which appeal to children. She has also written longer tales, books for adults and collections of folk tales.

HOURIHANE, URSULA. *Happy Go Lucky Stories*. Methuen.
Other collections and stories to read and tell by this author.

LINDGREN, ASTRID. *All About the Bullerby Children*. Puffin.
A delightful collection of tales about the Swedish village of Bullerby and the children who live there. Just one among a large number of very readable tales both for young children and those over 8.

PIERCE, PHILLIPPA. *Mrs Cockle's Cat*. Constable.
A long story about an old lady and her cat with lots happening.

PROYSEN, ALF. *Old Mrs Pepperpot*. Puffin.
There are lots of stories about this pleasant old lady who has an exciting way of shrinking to the size of a pepperpot.

REEVES, JAMES (ed.). *A Golden Land*. Stories from Hans Andersen, Walter De La Mare and others. Constable.
The Secret Shoemaker. Illustrated by Edward Ardizzone. Retells some of the Brothers Grimm's lesser known tales.
There are a number of other collections of tales by James Reeves as well as stories for older children.

ROBINSON, JOAN G. *Teddy Robinson's Omnibus*. Harrap.

RUSKIN, JOHN. *The King of the Golden River*. Allen and Unwin.
A moral tale of magic available in various editions, much enjoyed by children.

SAUNDERS, RUTH MANNING. *Oh Really Rabbit*. Methuen.
Just one of the many collections of all sorts of tales by Ruth Manning Saunders.

TOMLINSON, JILL. *The Owl Who Was Afraid of the Dark*. Methuen.
A lovely reading aloud tale – one of many by this author.

STORR, CATHERINE. *Clever Polly and the Stupid Wolf*. Puffin.
One of many tales by this author. One of my favourites; light-hearted and amusing.

WILDE, OSCAR. *The Selfish Giant*. Published by a variety of publishers.
A collection of stories much enjoyed by children. Some of the stories are obtainable singly in picture book form.

113

WILLIAMS, URSULA MORAY. *Adventures of the Little Wooden Horse.* Puffin.

All about a little horse who brings back a fortune when he goes to sell himself to help his master. A story to read aloud to the 5–8 years olds.

2 *Verse*

> *Poetry turns all things to loveliness.*
> Shelley

NURSERY RHYMES

There are so many books on nursery rhymes, and new ones are always appearing, so one can really take one's pick. Those mentioned here are just a few of the old favourites which are particularly loved and enjoyed.

BRIGGS, RAYMOND (ed.). *Ring A Ring O'Roses.* Hamish Hamilton.

GREENAWAY, KATE (illustrated). *Mother Goose.* Warne.

LINES, KATHLEEN (ed.). *Lavender's Blue.* OUP.
Illustrated by Harold Jones.

MATHERSON, ELIZABETH (compiler). *This Little Puffin Nursery Rhymes and Songs.* Penguin.

MONTGOMERIE, NORAH and WILLIAM (ed.). *Scottish Nursery Rhymes.* Hogarth Press.

OPIE, IONA (ed.). *Ditties for the Nursery.* OUP.
Illustrated by Monica Walter.

OPIE, IONA and PETER. *The Oxford Nursery Rhyme Book.* OUP.
Illustrated by Joan Hassall with early engravings and woodcuts.

OPIE, IONA and PETER. *The Oxford Dictionary of Nursery Rhymes.* OUP.
Illustrated with line and half tone reproductions.

OPIE, IONA and PETER. *The Puffin Book of Nursery Rhymes.* Penguin.
Pictures by Pauline Baynes.

POTTER, BEATRIX. *Cecily Parsley's Nursery Rhymes, Apple Dapply Nursery Rhymes.* Warne.

RACKHAM, ARTHUR. *Mother Goose Nursery Rhymes*. Pan Books.

STONES, ROSEMARY and MANN, ANDREW. *Mother Goose Comes to Cable Street*. Penguin.
Illustrated by Dan Jones.

TUCKER, NICHOLAS (collector). *Mother Goose Abroad*. Hamish Hamilton.
Pictures by Trevor Stobley.

WILDSMITH, BRIAN (ed.). *Mother Goose*. OUP.
A riot of lovely colour.

INDIVIDUAL AUTHORS

BAYLEY, NICOLA. *One Old Oxford Fox*. Jonathan Cape.
Lovely pictures by the author.

BELLOC, H. *Selected Cautionary Verses*. Puffin.
Various editions available.

BLAKE, WILLIAM. *Songs of Innocence and Experience*. Faber.
Various editions available.

BODECKER, N. M. *Let's Marry said the Cherry*. Faber.
Illustrated by the author.

BONNER, ANN and ROGER. *Earlybirds, Earlywords*. Abelard-Schuman.
Very short poems for the very young. Lots of pictures.

BROOKE, L. LESLIE. *The Johnny Crow Books*. Warne.

BROWNING, ROBERT. *The Pied Piper of Hamelin*. Editions by various publishers in picture book form.

LEWIS, CARROLL. *The Lobster Quadrille*. Warne.
Also *The Walrus and the Carpenter*. Illustrated by Tony Cattaneo. Other editions and poems available by other publishers. Poems no child should miss.

CAUSLEY, CHARLES. *Figgin Hobbin*. Puffin.
Collected Poems 1957–75. Macmillan.
Charles Causley has written many poems that children will enjoy.

115

DE LA MARE, WALTER. *Peacock Pie*. Faber.
Songs of Childhood, Secret Laughter. In paper and hardback in a variety of different editions.

ELIOT, T. S. *The Illustrated Old Possum*. Faber.
Illustrated by Nicolas Bentley. Available in various editions.

GRAVES, ROBERT. *The Penny Fiddle*. Cassell.
Illustrated by Edward Ardizzone.

GREENAWAY, KATE. *Selections from Marygold Garden*. Fontana Picture Lions.
Illustrated by the author. There are numerous other collections of Kate Greenaway's poems with her charming old-fashioned pictures.

HUGHES, TED. *Moonbells and Other Poems*. Chatto and Windus.
There are a number of other books of poetry by Ted Hughes in hardback and paperback which children will enjoy.

LEAR, EDWARD. *The Complete Nonsense of Edward Lear*. Edited by Holbrook Jackson. Warne.
No child should miss the enchanting and amusing poetry of Edward Lear. There are a variety of editions in hardback and paperback to choose from.

MILLIGAN, SPIKE. *A Book of Milliganimals*. Puffin.
Laughter provoking rhymes. Also *Silly Verse for Kids*.

MILNE, A.A. *When We Were Very Young*. Methuen.
Illustrated by Ernest Shepard. A. A. Milne's poetry needs no introduction – in paperback and hardback.

NASH, OGDEN. *Custard and Company*. Puffin.
Selected and illustrated by Quentin Blake. Really funny verse by this American poet.

REEVES, JAMES. *The Blackbird in the Lilac*. OUP.
Illustrated by Edward Ardizzone.
The Wandering Moon. Heinemann.
Complete Poems for Children (illustrated by Edward Ardizonne). Heinemann.

ROSEN, MICHAEL. *You Can't Catch Me*. André Deutch.
Illustrated by Quentin Blake.

ROSSETTI, CHRISTINA. *Sing Song*. Dover Constable.
Illustrated by Arthur Hughes. Simple but delightful poetry.

STEVENSON, ROBERT LOUIS. *A Child's Garden of Verse*. Puffin.
Also available in many other editions. A poet no child should
miss – about the experiences children themselves have.

There are many other individual poets, both those who are writing
today and those who have written things that young children still
enjoy i.e. Thomas Hardy, Keats, Shelley, Wordsworth, Dylan
Thomas, John Clare, just to mention a few but they will need
looking for.

ANTHOLOGIES

ADAM SMITH, JANE (ed.). *The Faber Book of Children's Verse*. Faber.
A very pleasing and useful collection.

AGAR, KENNETH (compiler). *Nothing Solemn*. Evans.

BAKER, TOM (compiler). *Never Wear Your Wellies in the House*.
Sparrow Books.
Illustrators (various). Poems to amuse.

BENNETT, JILL (compiler). *Days Are Where We Live*. Bodley Head.
Illustrated by Maureen Rolfey.
Tiny Tim Verses for Children. Illustrated by Helen Oxenbury.
Heinemann.

BERG, LEILA (ed.). *Four Feet and Two*. Penguin.
Decorations by Shirley Birk and Marvin Bileck. A delightful
collection about animals.

BOSWELL, HILDA (selector and illustrator). *Treasury of Poetry*. Collins.
Rather lush pictures and poems but quite pleasing.

BRANDRETH, GYLES. *What Nonsense*. Knight Books.
Illustrated by Ann Axworthy. Funny poems and cartoon like
pictures.

CALDECOTT, RANDOLPH. *Collection of Pictures and Songs*. Warne.
Illustrated by the author.

CASS, JOAN E. (ed.). *The Patchwork Quilt and other poems*. Longman.
Illustrated by William Stobbs.

CAUSLEY, CHARLES. *A Puffin Book of Magic Verse*. Puffin.
A very delightful collection for a variety of ages.

CHAMBERS, NANCY. *Stir About Rhymes from Then and Now*. Blackbird.
Illustrated by Carolyn Bull.

CLARK, LEONARD (ed.). *Drums and Trumpets*. Bodley Head.
Illustrated by Heather Copley.
Flutes and Cymbols. Bodley Head. Illustrated by Shirley Hughes.
Two useful collections. Leonard Clark, himself, has written a
number of poetry books which young children will enjoy about
everyday happenings.

COLE, WILLIAM. *Oh What Nonsense*. Methuen.
Illustrated by Toni Ungerer. Amusing and ridiculous rhymes.

CRANE, WALTER. *The Baby's Opera*. Warne.

DE LA MARE, WALTER. *Come Hither*. Puffin and Kestrel.
Illustrated by Diana Bloomfield. Old-fashioned but very
endearing.

DOWNIE, MARY ALICE and ROBERTSON, BARBARA (compilers). *The
Wind Has Wings. Poems from Canada*. OUP.
Illustrated by Elizabeth Cleaver.
A charming collection, mainly for older children but very
worthwhile.

GRAHAM, ELEANOR (ed.). *A Puffin Quartet of Poets*. Puffin.
(Eleanor Farjeon, James Reeves, E. V. Riev, Ian Serraillier)
A very useful and endearing collection for all ages.

HENDRA, JUDITH. *The Illustrated Treasury*. Hodder and Stoughton.
Humour for children. Various illustrators.

IRESON, BARBARA. *Rhyme Time*. Hamlyn Beaver Books.
Illustrated by Lesley Smith.

The Faber Book of Nursery Verse. Illustrated by George Smith. Just two of the numerous collections by Barbara Ireson.

LISTER, DAPHNE. *Gingerbread Pigs and Other Rhymes*. Carousel. Illustrated by Caroline McDonald Paul. A delightful picture paperback.

READ, HERBERT. *This Way Delight*. Faber. Illustrated by Charles Stewart.

SCOTT MITCHELL, CLARE. *When a Goose Meets a Mouse*. Evans. Illustrated by Louise Hogan.

THWAITE, ANN (ed.). *All Sorts of Poems*. Methuen. Illustrated by Patricia Mullins.

WATERS, FIONA. *Out of the Blue*. Fontana Picture Lions. An anthology of weather poems. Drawings and etchings by Veroni. A really lovely collection.

WATSON, JULIA (chosen). *The Armada Book of Young Verse*. Collins. Illustrated by Quentin Blake. Also *A Children's Zoo* (Fontana Lions). Illustrated by Karen Strachey.

3 Background books

Some books are to be Tasted, others are to be swallowed, and some few to be Chewed and Digested; that is, some books are to be Read but not curiously; and some few to be Read Wholly and with Diligence and Attention.
Francis Bacon

(OP – denotes Out of Print; but the title is usually available from libraries)

AITKEN, JOAN. *The Way To Write for Children*. Elm Tree Books 1982.

ARIES, PHILIPPA. *Centuries of Childhood*. Cape 1962.

BETTELHEIM, BRUNO. *The Uses of Enchantment. The Meaning and Importance of Fairy Tales*. Thames and Hudson 1976.

BLISHEN, EDWARD (ed.). *The Thorney Paradise. Writers on Writing for Children*. Kestrel Books 1975.

BLOUNT, MARGARET. *Animal Land*. Hutchinson 1974.

BUTLER, DOROTHY. *Babies Need Books*. Bodley Head 1980.

CHAMBERS, AIDAN. *Introducing Books to Children*. Heinemann Educational 1973.

CHUKOVSKY, KORNEI. *From Two to Five*. Translated and edited by Miriam Morton. University of California Press 1966.

CLODD, EDWARD. *Tom Tit Tot*. Duckworth 1968. OP

CROUCH, M. *The Whole World Story Book*. OUP 1983.

ECOFF, SHEILA; STUBBS, G. T. and ASHLEY, L. F. (ed.). *Only Connect. Readings in Children's Literature*. OUP 1969.

FADER, DANIEL and MCNEIL, ELTON B. *Hooked on Books*. Pergamon 1966.

FISHER, MARGERY. *Intent Upon Reading* (1961), *Matters of Fact* (1972). Hodder and Stoughton.

FORD, B. (ed.). *Young Writers, Young Readers*. Hutchinson 1963. OP

FRAIGBERG, SELMA H. *The Magic Years*. Charles Scribner's Sons 1959.

FRAZER, JAMES. *The Golden Bough*. Macmillan 1925. Available in other editions.

FREEMAN, GILLIAN. *The Undergrowth of Literature. Books and Magazines*. Nelson 1967.

FREUD, ANNA. *The Ego and the Mechanism of Defence*. Hogarth Press 1954.

FREUD, SIGMUND. *Totem and Taboo 1919*. (Translated by J. Strachey.) Routledge 1950.

GESELL, ARNOLD and ILG, FRANCIS I. *The Child from Five to Ten. Infant and Child in the Culture of Today*. Hamish Hamilton 1946.

FROMM, ERIC. *The Forgotten Language*. Gollancz 1952.

GOLDMAN, RONALD. *Religious Thinking, From Childhood to Adolescence*. RKP 1964.

GOMME, G. L. (ed.). *The Handbook of Folklore.* London Folklore Society 1980. OP

GREENE, GRAHAM. *The Lost Childhood and Other Essays.* Penguin 1962.

GRUGEON, ELIZABETH and WALDEN, PETER. *Literature and Learning.* (Open University Set Book) Ward Lock 1978.

HARTLEY, RUTH; LAWRENCE, FRANK and GOLDERSON, R. M. *Understanding Children's Play.* RKP 1953.

HAZARD, PAUL. *Books, Children and Men.* 4th edn. Boston Horn Book 1960.

HAZLITT, WILLIAM. *Lectures on the English Poets.* (various publishers)

HEEKS, PEGGY. *Ways of Knowing. Information Books for 7 to 9 years.* A Signal Guidebook 1983.

HILDICK, E. WALLACE. *Children and Fiction.* 2nd edn. Evans 1974.

HOGGART, RICHARD. *The Uses of Literacy.* Chatto and Windus 1957.

ISAACS, SUSAN. *Intellectual Growth in Young Children.* RKP 1930.
Social Development in Young Children. RKP 1933.
Childhood and After. RKP 1948.

LEE, R. S. *Psychology and Worship.* SCM Press 1958. OP
Your Growing Child and Religion. Penguin 1965. OP

LEWIS, C DAY. *Poetry for You.* Blackwell 1946. OP

MARSHALL, MARGARET and MARSHALL, R. *An Introduction to Children's Books.* Gower 1983.

MEAD, MARGARET. *Learning to Read.* Bodley Head 1983.

MONEY-KYRLE, R. *Superstition and Society.* Hogarth Press 1930. OP

MOSS, ELAINE. *The Good Book Guide to Children's Books.* Penguin 1983.

OPIE, IONA and PETER. *The Lore and Language of School Children.* OUP 1959.

PIAGET, JEAN. *The Moral Judgement of the Child.* RKP 1932.
The Language and Thought of the Child. RKP 1920.

REID, FORREST. *Milk of Paradise*. Faber 1946. OP

RHOEIM, C. *The Riddle of the Sphinx*. Hogarth Press 1934. OP

RUSKIN, JOHN. *Sesame and Lilies, The Two Paths*. Allen and Unwin 1933.

SAMPSON, GEORGE. *Seven Essays*. CUP 1947. OP

SAWYER, RUTH. *The Way of the Storyteller*. Bodley Head 1966. OP

SHEDLOCK, MARIE L. *The Art of the Storyteller*. (rev. edn.) Dover Publications 1951. OP

SHERIDAN, MARY D. *The Developmental Progress of Infants and Young Children*. HMSO 1960.

SMITH, J. W. D. *Psychology and Religion in Early Childhood*. SCM Press. OP

SMITH, LILIAN H. *The Unreluctant Years*. Chicago University Press 1950.

SOUTHALL, IVAN. *A Journey of Discovery*. Kestrel 1975.

STAVILAND, VIRGINIA. *Children and Literature. Views and Reviews*. Bodley Head 1973.

STONEY, BARBARA. *A Biography, Enid Blyton*. Hodder and Stoughton 1974. OP

TERMAN, R. LARS and MERRILL, MAUD. *Measuring Intelligence*. Harrap 1937.

THOMPSON, FRANCES. *Shelley*. Burns & Oates 1923.

TUCKER, NICHOLAS (ed.). *The Child and the Book*. CUP 1983.

VERNEY, THOMAS and KELLY, JOHN. *The Secret Life of the Unborn Child*. Sphere Books 1982.

VERNON, M. D. *The Psychology of Perception*. Penguin 1962.

WHITE, DOROTHY. *About Books for Children*. OUP 1948. OP
Books Before Five. OUP 1954. OP

SOME HELPFUL BOOKS ON SEX EDUCATION FOR YOUNG CHILDREN

ALTHEA. *A Baby in the Family.* (illustrated) Dinosaur 1975.
Written in relation to the family and concerned with happy, warm relationships.

GRUENBERG, SIDONIE MATSNER. *How you were Born.* World's Work 1973.
A useful book for the sixes and sevens.

HANSSON, GUNILLA and FAGERSTROM, GRETHE. *Our New Baby.* (illustrated) Macdonald 1980.
A book for parents and children to read together.

JARNER, BO. *My New Sister.* A and C Black 1977.
A story in photographs for the 3–6 year olds, pleasing and simple.

KNUDSEN, PER HOLM. *How a Baby is Made.* Pan 1975.
Shows in text and humorous pictures how a baby is conceived and born.

MAYLE, PETER. *Where Did I Come From.* Macmillan 1978.
The facts of life clearly portrayed with illustrations.

RAYNER, CLAIRE. *The Body Book.* (illustrated) Piccolo 1979.
Tells how the body works from birth to dying.

SPIERS, HILARY. *How You Began.* (illustrated) Dent 1971.
All about bodies, babies and parents.

Picture Books

ADAMS, J. and G. *Topsy and Tim's Thursday Book.* Blackie.
A baby is born next door and their mother goes in to help.

WOLDE, GUNILLA. *Thomas is Different.* Hodder and Stoughton.
English text by Alison Winn. A charming picture of a small boy and girl playing together.

REVIEWS AND PERIODICALS

Books for Your Children. (editor Anne Wood), 90 Gillhurst Road,

Harborne, Birmingham 17.
Directed to parents particularly. (3 issues a year.)

Books for Keeps. (editor Pat Trigg), 1 Effinham Road, Lee, London
SE12 8NZ. (6 issues a year.)
School Bookshop Association. Particularly for parents and
teachers.

Children's Literature in Education. An international quarterly (editor
Mrs Barbara Collinge), 2 Sunwine Place, Exmouth, Devon.

Growing Point. (editor Margery Fisher), Ashton Manor,
Northampton NN7 2JL. (6 issues a year.)

Junior Bookshelf. (editor Diana Morrell), Marsh Hall, Thurston-
land, Huddersfield, Yorkshire. (6 issues a year.)

Signal. (editor Nancy Chambers), Thimble Press, Lockwood,
Station Road, South Woodchester, Gloucestershire GL5 5EQ.
(3 issues a year.)

SOCIETIES AND INSTITUTIONS

School Library Association, Victoria House, 29–31 George Street,
Oxford OX1 2AY.

The National Book League, Book House, 45 East Hill, London
SW8 2OZ.
Publishes book lists, arranges exhibitions, provides book infor-
mation etc.

British Association for Early Childhood Education, Montgomery
Hall, Kennington Oval, London SE11 5SW.
Provides information on the needs of young children.

Pollocks Toy Museum, 1 Scala Street, London W1.
Children's toy theatres. Can be bought for children to cut out
and put together.

Federation of Children's Book Group, 22 Beacon Brow, Bradford
BD6 3DE. Secretary Martin Kromer.

Appendix

Childhood Books in Autobiography
My childhood leans beside me.

Perhaps it is only in childhood that books have any deep influence in our lives. In later life we admire, we are entertained, we may modify some views we already hold, but we are more likely to find in books merely a confirmation of what is in our minds already: as in a love affair it is our own features that we see reflected back.

But in childhood all books are books of divination, telling us about the future, and like the fortune teller who sees a long journey in the cards or death by water they influence the future.

I suppose that is why books excited us so much. What do we ever get nowadays from reading to equal the excitement and the revelation in those first fourteen years?

I remember distinctly the suddenness with which a key turned in a lock and I found I could read – not just the sentences in a reading book with syllables coupled like railway carriages, but a real book.

All a long summer holiday I kept my secret as I believed: I did not want anyone to know that I could read. I suppose I half consciously realized even then that this was the dangerous moment. I was safe so long as I could read – the wheels had begun to turn, but now the future stood around on bookshelves everywhere waiting for a child to choose.

> *Collected Essays*. Graham Greene. The Bodley Head 1969.

The second glimpse came through *Squirrel Nutkin*, through it only, though I loved all the Beatrix Potter books. But the rest of them were merely entertaining, it administered the shock, it was a trouble. It troubled me with what I can only describe as the idea of Autumn. It sounds fantastic to say that one can be enamoured of a season, but that is something like what happened, and as before, the experience was one of intense desire. And one that went back to the book not to

125

gratify the desire (that was impossible – how can one possess Autumn?) but to reawake it. And in this experience also the same surprise and the same sense of incalculable importance.

It was something quite different from ordinary life and even from ordinary pleasure, something they would now say, 'in another dimension'.

Surprised by Joy. C. S. Lewis. Geoffrey Bliss 1959.

It was she (my mother) who guided the first tentative probings of my mind and taught me to read by the time I was five – first Beatrix Potter, then Winnie the Pooh and the now almost forgotten Olwen Bowen farmyard books peopled by Hepzibah Hen and Gertie Grunter, to be followed soon by Helen's Babies.

And it was through my mother's eyes that I saw all this, for until I could snatch these delights for myself she was the sole interpreter and guide to the magic world that lay imprisoned inside the words.

To me who had never stirred beyond a mile of our garden it was rather as if the authors had been part of the scene and had woven the stories around it for me alone. The cabbage patch that Beatrix Potter drew was our cabbage patch where old Mr Wade wheezed over his spade with a robin in attendance. And weren't the six Corsican Pines that stood on the heath half a mile away on a knoll carpeted with gorse, the same pine trees where Winnie the Pooh met his friends. I only knew the fantasy took hold of me so completely that for months I hauled my long suffering teddy bear to the spot every afternoon in the hope that we should surprise Piglet and Pooh at a tea party.

I shall never forget the day when I tried to explain something of this to cousin Ethel who was staying with us, she was all good deeds for others and a tongue that dripped vinegar.

'That's story book stuff,' she said, 'and it sounds to me as if you were filling your head with rubbish.'

Just then my mother came into the room and you should have seen her face as she heard.

'It seems to me,' she said, and her words were like sharp stones, 'that God gave a child its imagination to be used.'

A House Called Memory. Richard Collier. Collins 1960.

The best moment of the week was the arrival of the weekly comic *Puck*, one penny, not a mere halfpenny comic like *Chips*, but *Puck* which had just started to have two pages in actual colours never quite fitting the lines – a fact which used to distress me when it was bad enough to diminish the reality of my favourite characters. Sometimes I'd start waiting at four-thirty though *Puck* wasn't due to arrive till five; and before the interminable half hour was over I would have had to go upstairs to look at my new celluloid dolphin. And then there was *Puck*, lying on the doormat, new and stinking spendidly of cheap printer's ink.

'Father!'

The legs of grown-ups seems to push through treacle just when there is most need to hurry. Soon I was on his knee in his study and there amid the smell of cigarettes lighted, cigarette recently grown cold and stubs gone dry with age, he would work through every page of it for me. Saved for the last were the Adventures of Professor Radium, the inventor who discovered ways of peeling bananas by electrical x-rays. . . . How marvellous to be read to. Father seemed to enjoy it as much as I did.

> *Steps to Maturity.* Stephen Polter's autobiography. Rupert Hart
> Davis 1959.

If the charm of Nursie's stories were that they were always the same, so that Nursie represented the rock of stability in my life, the charm of my mother was that her stories were always different. One story I remember was about a mouse called Bright Eyes. Bright Eyes had several different adventures, but suddenly, one day, to my dismay, my mother declared that there were no more stories about Bright Eyes to tell. I was on the point of weeping when my mother said: 'But I'll tell you a story about a Curious Candle.' We had two instalments of the Curious Candle, which was, I think, a kind of detective story, when unluckily some visitors came to stay and our private games and stories were in abeyance. When the visitors left and I demanded the end of the Curious Candle, which had paused at a most thrilling moment when the villain was slowly rubbing poison into the candle, my mother looked blank and apparently could remember nothing about the matter. That unfinished serial

127

still haunts my mind.

Agatha Christie. An Autobiography. Collins 1977.

When I was a very little child, I used to amuse myself and my brothers with inventing stories, such as I read. Having, as I suppose, naturally a restless mind and busy imagination, this soon became the chief pleasure of my life.

I had not known there was any harm in it, until Miss Shore (a Calvinist governess) finding it out lectured me most severely, and told me it was wicked.

From that time forth I considered that to invent a story of any kind was a sin. But the desire to do so was too deeply rooted in my affections to be resisted in my own strength ... The longing to invent stories grew with violence; everything I heard or read became food for my distemper.

My own state, however was, I should think, almost unique among the children of cultivated parents. In consequence of the stern ordinance which I have described, not a single fiction was read or told to me during my infancy. The rapture of the child who delays the process of going to bed by cajoling 'a story' out of his mother or his nurse, as he sits upon her knee, well tucked up, at the corner of the nursery fire – this was unknown to me. Never in all my early childhood did anyone address to me the affecting preamble, 'Once upon a time'. I was told about missionaries, but never about pirates: I was familiar with hummingbirds, but I had never heard of fairies. Jack the Giant Killer, Rumpelstiltskin, and Robin Hood were not of my aquaintance, and though I understood about wolves, Little Red Riding Hood was a stranger even by name ...

Having easily said what in those early years I did not read I have great difficulty in saying what I did read. But a queer variety of natural history, some of it quite indigestible by my undeveloped mind; many books of travels, mainly of a scientific character, among them voyages of discovery in the South Seas, by which my brain was dimly filled with splendour.

Father and Son. Edmund Gosse. Heinemann 1907.

'Willie read indiscriminately. I had a strong preference for school stories and above all for the penny weeklies, the *Gem* and the *Magnet*. Their appeal to me was that the characters in them were getting a really good education and that some of it was bound to brush off on me.'

Frank O'Connor's mother went out to work and as at some houses she did half a day Frank was allowed into the kitchen before she had finished work.

'I was not only admitted to the big warm kitchen after school and given my tea, but if the family was out I was allowed to accompany Mother upstairs while she did the bedrooms or go to the lumber room in the attic which was chock full of treasures, old pamphlets, guide books, phrase books in French and German, old dance programmes from Vienna and Munich – and the greatest prize of all an illustrated book of the Oberammergen Passion Play with the text in German and English. It was junk that would not have meant anything to anyone else but for me it was "the right twigs for an eagle's nest" … It filled my mind with images of how educated people lived.'

An Only Child. Frank O'Connor. Macmillan 1961, Pan 1970.

I began my life as I shall no doubt end it: among books. In my grandfather's study, they were everywhere; it was forbidden to dust them except once a year, before the October term. Even before I could read, I already revered those raised stones; upright or leaning, wedged together like bricks on the library shelves or nobly spaced like avenues of dolmans, I felt that our family prosperity depended on them. They were all alike, and I was romping about in a tiny sanctuary, surrounded by squat, ancient monuments which had witnessed my birth, which would witness my death and whose permanence guaranteed me a future as calm as my past. I used to touch them in secret to honour my hands with their dust but I did not have much idea what to do with them and each day I was present at ceremonies whose meaning escaped me: my grandfather – so clumsy, normally, that my grandmother buttoned his gloves for him – handled these cultural objects with the dexterity of an officiating priest. Hundreds of times I saw him get up absent-mindedly, walk round the table, cross the room in two strides, unhesitatingly pick out a volume without allowing himself time for choice, then run through it as he went back to his armchair, with a combined movement of his thumb and right forefinger, and almost before he sat down, open it with a flick 'at the right page', making it creak like a shoe. I sometimes got close enough to observe these boxes which opened like oysters and I discovered the nakedness of their internal organs, pale, dank, slightly blistered pages, covered with small black veins, which drank ink and smelt of mildew.

I Loathe my Childhood and all that remains of it ... Words. Jean-Paul Sartre. Penguin 1967.